Remembering Me

Karl Scott Pat

by
Nancy Green

Order this book online at www.trafford.com
or email orders@trafford.com

Most Trafford titles are also available at major online book retailers.

Printed in Victoria, BC, Canada.

ISBN: 978-1-4269-2847-5 (sc)
ISBN: 978-1-4269-2981-6 (eb)

*Our mission is to efficiently provide the world's finest, most comprehensive book publishing
service, enabling every author to experience success. To find out how to publish your
book, your way, and have it available worldwide, visit us online at www.trafford.com*

Trafford rev. 3/29/10

 www.trafford.com

North America & international
toll-free: 1 888 232 4444 (USA & Canada)
phone: 250 383 6864 ♦ fax: 812 355 4082

*I*T'S DECEMBER 2009 AS I begin this saga. I want to record things for my kids & grandkids to have when I am no longer here. It's not my intention that this be perfect, or that it be made into a movie. It originated on tape, but now I'm trying to put it into words to read. I'm not too sure that everything is really a memory, because although some things I know I've experienced; it may be that I've been told other things that *seem* to be a memory. I have talked to my brother, Dwight, on some occasions, & we have "remembered" things together – although, sometimes it seems our memories are not quite the same. I just finished reading his book that he had printed about himself for his grandkids, & that's when I decided to put my own thoughts, (taped & otherwise) on paper. I'm going to begin by transcribing the tapes & perhaps stick other things in as I remember them.

As you well know, I always have an opinion & very seldom keep it to myself, so this will be my version of what I remember or what was told to me. There may be things in these stories that you remember differently, but that's because we are all different & interpret things differently. One thing that I do remember is that my mother loved me & I hope that you remember that I loved you too.

These thoughts may not be in chronological order, but they are going to be written in the order they kick in to my memories. The first thing I remember, is that when I was very young – I don't remember how young, but had to be under 8 yrs old, as it was when we lived in Old Dearborn. I remember making tents out of blankets in the alley & playing house. We used to eat beans on little plates. Other things of that early time I think are things I've been told rather than memories.

I didn't know my dad until I became a teenager. He was born May 28, 1907 & raised in Almo, Kentucky on a farm with Granddad Patton & Grandmother Patton. Granddad was a redhead, kind of roly-poly and he smoked Marvel cigarettes. Grandmother Patton was tall, thin & she always wore her hair pulled back tied up in a bun at the nape of her neck. She always wore long-sleeved cotton dresses that went down to her ankles. She wore "ball" shoes as they were called then. Actually they were high top sneakers. On Sundays when she went to church, she wore regular shoes. I don't remember her ever going anywhere but to church. Granddad was the one who went to town to sell milk or cream, or whatever & to buy staples.

When I was 14 yrs old I spent the summer in KY & I remember Grandmother Patton sitting in a rocker on the front porch, brushing her hair & it went all the way down to the floor. I asked her how she could possibly wash it being that long. She said she had never washed it & that so long as you didn't wash it, brushing it was sufficient. She would then twist it & turn it into the bun at the back of her neck. At that same time we were sitting on the porch & talking, & I was interested in getting some background on my family. I asked Granddad about ancestry. Asked where everyone was from. He told me he was Irish-German & when I asked about Grandmother, he said she was Indian. When I asked him what kind of Indian, he said "Indian Indian" kind of angrily, & I just let it go at the time. Later on, I have come to believe in talking to people & researching that it was possibly, Cherokee. There is a book somewhere, written by Christine Patton (one of Dad's cousins) on the history of the Turnbows. That was Grandmother's maiden name.

I remember that Grandma Patton (Jay) called me when you guys were just little & we lived on the farm in Posen asking for information for Christine & the book she was getting printed on the Turnbows. Looking back now, it is possible that it wasn't really a book, but more likely research into the ancestry. I have also done some research on the family & found that there was an Isaac Turnbow who married Margaret Tallkitten, and from those names, I would have to assume there was American Indian in there somewhere. Although, when I asked Uncle J I about it, he said he didn't recall any Indian in the family. There was, though, a distinctive nose on that side of the family, which seemed to infer an Indian background. We jokingly called it the "Turnbow Hump".

Anyway, that summer that I spent in KY, I found out more about my family than I had known before. My mother was Trema Lillian Filbeck, born May 13, 1909 and she married my Dad, Orvice Monroe Patton, on Feb 27, 1926 & later they divorced. He was born on May 28, 1907. She filed for divorce in March of 1934 & it was final August 6, 1935. So long as I'm on names, I will tell you that Granddad Patton was Willard Oetis Patton. He went by his initials W.O., but I do remember Grandmother Patton calling him Oetis rather than the W.O. everyone else referred to. Her name was Hattie. I'm not positive if her middle name was Jane, but I believe the Jane in my name came from the Pattons. Grandmother Filbeck was Nancy & I got my name from her. Granddad Filbeck was Lonnie Filbeck. Lonnie was a big man – not fat, but tall. He wore bib overalls & was a farmer. It didn't seem that either one of my Granddads worked very hard; while it did seem the women in both families were hard workers. This may be just how I saw it. I know Granddad Filbeck was some kind of Township or County Officer, & I also remember him raising strawberries. Granddad Patton had tobacco, then some kind of hybrid popcorn, & I also remember molasses cane.

The Filbecks lived in Hardin, KY. Grandmother Filbeck (Miss Nancy) seemed to be a character. She loved joking. She had black hair parted in the middle with grey streaks. She also wore her hair in a bun at the nape of her neck. She was a pretty woman, except that she had hair on her face, in a mustache & on the chin. That seems to have been hereditary - I have the same. I remember that when I was about 10 yrs old, my mother said that if I did get the hair on the face she would have it removed by electrolysis. Of course, she didn't live to see me after the hair began to grow. Grandmother's maiden name was Magness. When I was there I also asked Granddad Filbeck about the ancestry. He said he was also German-Irish & that Grandmother was Dutch. At the time I took it to mean Holland Dutch; but thinking about it later, I think it was German "Dutch". He told me that their ancestors came over on the same boat. I have just lately learned that his great-great-great grandfather was born in Wiesbaden, Germany in 1728. His name was Wilhelm Ernst Felbach. Obviously, the spelling of the name has changed. The year I was 14, I decided that I was ¼ Dutch, ¼ German, ¼ Irish & ¼ Cherokee Indian.

I'll tell you a little funny story about the "Indian" part. As I said, I was 14 that summer & in the fall, I went to my first year in High School at Cooley in Detroit. I had a World History class & we were studying ancestries & Indonesia, etc. The teacher was discussing this and talking about India Indians. I thought of Indians from India as being rather exotic, & never thought of them as being black, or Negro. At any rate, the teacher asked the kids about their ancestry. I thought about my Granddad telling me my grandmother was "Indian Indian", & I figured I wasn't exactly lying, & I really wanted to have an exotic ancestry, so when the teacher came to me (& I was in the front row), after the other kids had mentioned either German, English, Italian, etc., I said I was ¼ Irish, ¼ German, ¼ Dutch & ¼ Indian. She immediately asked "What kind of Indian" –

my opportunity, right? I replied "India Indian". Then as she went further on & came to the blacks in the class, they were almost all Indian or Indonesian also. Then, I wasn't so proud of it!

To get back to my ancestry – yours; Trema & Orvice (my mom & dad) were married when she was only 16 or 17 yrs. Old, & he wasn't much older. They were married in Kentucky, but she had gone to school. I don't think Dad finished school. I have her certificate of completion of the Eighth Grade & promotion to high school. I believe she went on to Murray State; although I don't think she finished. Aunt Lois did teach & told me that my mother also did some substitute teaching. At any rate, she was very young when she married.

I also heard that she played with "paper dolls" before having any kids. I do remember playing "paper dolls" from catalogs myself. We would cut out pictures in the catalogs & play house with them. Later, these paper dolls were replaced with those we cut out of books that were actually printed for that purpose, with separate clothes that could be put on the dolls. We used oatmeal boxes, round ones & rectangular ones to make up the houses & furniture for our paper dolls.

The rest of the catalog could be put to good use as toilet paper in the outhouse. I never saw the house that they lived in & where Dwight was born. It was around the corner from the Filbecks & that is also gone now, taken by a tornado in much later years.

One of the things I remember about the house, both granddads' houses, was the porch.

The Pattons was a larger house, with a porch around & in front. There was a screened-in area in the back & they had the luxury of a well in that screened area. The well was similar to those in pictures you have seen, bricks raised above the floor with its own roof & pulleys attached to a bucket for getting water. Also, they kept their butter & things that needed cooling in a bucket in the water, or on a brick ledge inside the well.

The milk separated & the cream was put in a wooden churn with a paddle & the paddle would be pushed up & down until the cream would curdle & become butter. You could then scrape the butter off; salt it for flavoring, and the milk left was "buttermilk", which was very popular. I remember Uncle Burl loved to put chunks of cornbread into a glass of buttermilk & eat it with a spoon before going to bed. He had an ulcer & he said it was good for him.

But, I digress – Another thing that was typical of the houses, was a connected smokehouse. Granddad Patton's was off the enclosed porch – with a plank running from the porch to the smokehouse. Within the smokehouse, there were hams, sausage, & other "cured" meats hanging there. There was no refrigeration, so this was the way they were able to keep the meats. They were generally in mesh bags. Also there were home-canned goods stored there. Grandmother Filbeck's house had a smaller screened-in area, but she also had the plank to the Smokehouse.

They used a wood cook stove, & in the cupboard was a flour bin...they kept flour in it – usually a wooden bowl kept there. They would sift flour & other ingredients into the bowl & then flour on the enamel countertop, roll out the biscuits, etc., and cut them there. As I recall, all of the cooking was done early in the morning, since the heat from the wood stove would make it too hot in the house later, at least in the summer. I was never down there in the winter, so I don't know if it was different then. Grandmother Patton would get up at about 3 a.m., put the biscuits in, etc., and then go out & milk the cows, & come back in to put breakfast on the table, so that Granddad would have everything ready for him when he came in from his chores, whatever they were. There was usually chicken, and/or sausage, biscuits, gravy, & I remember fresh tomatoes. The milk gravy was made in the pan after the chicken or sausage was cooked, with milk being stirred in with flour thickening. We also had what was called "red-eye" gravy. It was made in the pan where smoked ham had been fried. Water was added to the red-colored cracklings. When put in a bowl, the grease would come to the top & biscuits were "sopped" in it. After breakfast, the plates, etc., were cleared & a table-cloth put over the table & it was left for the next meal.

Back to Grandmother Filbeck's house – it was much smaller than the Patton's. I don't remember that there was any living room – but each of the rooms was a bedroom, with a rocker, etc. for sitting. And, there was a central fireplace, making it possible to have fireplace heat in each of the individual bedrooms. There was an outside door in each of the bedrooms, leading to the porch. It was necessary to go out to the outhouse. The funny thing is I don't remember an outhouse at Grandmother Patton's. I don't know why, I know it was there, I just don't remember it. At night when you had to get up & go pee, you'd just go outside, off the porch & pee on the grass. I remember the outhouse at the Filbeck's, but I also remember that the chicken coop was closer & I remember that we just squatted in the chicken coop rather than go to the outhouse. At the Filbeck's it was a smaller house. Off the kitchen there was a closed stairway that went up to the attic. There was a long table in the middle of the kitchen. She had an interesting cupboard with a drawer that pulled out & she kept her eggs in that drawer. When the peddler came around, she would trade eggs for sewing material. I would get stick candy, & sometime, he even had what we called "nigger toes" –

a chocolate drop. There were shelves in the cupboard for pies, etc. I think it was called a "safe".

One time that summer when I was there, Grandmother asked if I liked onions & of course, I said I did. Then when we sat down to supper, the vegetable was onions. They were small, round onions, boiled. Other than the kitchen there were 3 small bedrooms, one off the kitchen & you had to go through one to get to the other. In the front bedroom there was an organ – the kind where you had to work the foot pedals to make it play. I believe it was oak. She told me that I could have it if I wanted it – I always thought it would be mine, but I guess other cousins thought the same thing. I have no idea what happened to it. Also, there was a fireplace & on the mantel she kept an old phonograph record which had been heated, fluted to make a bowl in which she kept her tobacco. She had 2 kinds. They raised their own tobacco; it was harvested, hung to dry in the barns, where fires were burned to cure it. The leaves were twisted into what was called a "twist" & then combined with a cut piece of "sweet" tobacco. The twist was too strong to be chewed by itself. The "sweet" tobacco came from the peddler. I remember that she could sit in the swing on the porch & spit that tobacco juice right over the porch & not a drop would fall.

Before we were married, Dick & I went to KY with Dwight & Jane, when Grandmother Patton was very ill. Grandmother Filbeck was always up to some kind of joking, & she kind of liked him. She asked if he smoked – he said yes & she said well, I guess it can't be too bad because she chewed. He said he chewed too (actually, he was talking about the Copenhagen snuff he put in his lower lip). She got a twinkle in her eye & asked if he would like to try her chew. She reached up into the molded record she kept her tobacco in & gave him a twist (leaving out the sweet part). He turned kind of green, but he wouldn't admit how bad it was.

The Filbeck well was outside in the yard. There were plum trees, peach trees & grape vines. There was also a big black iron kettle which hung over a fire pit which she used for washing clothes. She made her own lye soap for washing clothes...she just shaved off pieces into the boiling water. She used a stick to move the clothes around. She had a couple of big galvanized tubs, filled with cold water – when she took the clothes out of the boiling soapy water with a stick, she would just hold them up until most of the water dripped off, put into the first tub, moving them around for rinsing, etc., then they would go through a hand wringer into the second tub of cold water, where they were rinsed once more, then through the wringer, and onto the clothes line.

There were blue plums & also a tree with sweet plums – they were kind of yellow. She canned these plums & drinking the juice of those plums was like drinking brandy. They really became fermented when canned.

Granddad Filbeck's brother was known to us as Uncle Ottie & was married to aunt Bertha. They lived in the Dearborn/ Detroit area too. I remember that their food was kept cool in a window box. I later learned that his name was not Ottie, but Lottie – there were 4 brothers, Lonnie, Lottie, Lou & the fourth was Solon. We had an icebox. It wasn't electric, just a box with 2 parts. The top part was for putting in big chunks of ice, which melted slowly into a pan at the bottom, which had to be emptied as it became full. The ice was delivered to the apartments or houses by horse & wagon. I always wondered where the ice came from & didn't find until much later that there were companies (for example, in Alpena there was a Woodkowski Ice Co.) who went out onto the frozen lakes in the winter time & cut out the big chunks & then stored them in straw to keep them frozen. Anyway, Uncle Lottie was the only relative I remember of Granddad Filbeck. Grandmother had a brother named Zack. His name was probably Zachary. I don't remember anything about him, but I always associated his name with the movie star, Zachary Taylor.

I have looked up & found some family tree stuff since the computer. But that's not a part of this story.

Dwight was born in Kentucky, and then Dad went to Detroit to work for Henry Ford, as did most of the southern young men. I don't remember too much about the early life in Dearborn. Aunt Lois told me that when my mother was pregnant with me that she had problems & that dad went somewhere else for sex. When mom found out about it, it was something she couldn't forgive, & she divorced him. That apparently, was when dad met Jay whom he later married. I don't remember anything about it - & have only what Aunt Lois has told me.

Going back to the memories; I remember one time walking down the street with my uncle Frank; he was married to Aunt Dixie. I remember holding onto his hand, in an area near the viaduct where the rouge plant was & the bridge opened. I don't know if it is real or not – but it seems I saw a car hanging over the upper open bridge. This may have something to do with my current fear of bridges.

We once lived in a basement apartment, & I had pneumonia – I think that may have been a reason for moving. I also seem to remember an upstairs apartment where the couch was across a window – It seems I was sitting on the top of the couch looking out the window. Dwight was older than me & I think he was left to take care of me while mom worked.

Mom had a very good friend, Opal Albright, married to Uriel Albright, with a son Uriel, Jr., little older than Dwight. It may have been that Dwight was led to believe he was in charge, but that Opal was actually keeping an eye on us.

Mom worked at Turnstedt automobile factory. I remember that my Dad did send a check for $10 a week – whether that was for each of us or both until we were 18; however, she died before that & we eventually went to live with him. I believe she used that $10 to buy things for us. It's very vague, but I remember a puppy & Dwight & I taking him to a pet show, or something. This is very vague, because other than taking it to a pet show; I don't ever remember having a dog at that time.

Had a cousin, Laura June Filbeck, Uncle Joe's second oldest daughter. I don't remember this, but it is something I was told. Supposedly, Laura climbed up on a couch & fell out a 2nd story window – probably at 2 yrs. Old & probably suffered some kind of brain damage. She was always very nice & came to visit me one time when we were living at Grand Lake. I think she was on some kind of bowling trip at the time & found that I lived near so she just stopped to visit.

Sometime when mom was working at Turnstedt, she met Kelly Barker. I don't remember him from that time, at all, but I understand that he was a rather dapper young man. He had a "blind pig" illegal bar during prohibition. He appeared to have money at that time & was good looking, & I would think that mom needed someone to help with the 2 kids she had - at any rate they got married. I don't remember any of that, but my memories go to the house on Middlebelt road, where we moved after they got married. I believe Dwight was a big help in building the house. I remember it as having a red-brick artificial siding, a living room, dining room, kitchen & a bedroom. Kelly went to work for Bendix (also known as the "bomber plant"), which was out towards Ann Arbor. The Albrights lived on one side of us, & the Don Skivers lived on the other. It seems to me that Albright's was a beautiful southern type house & they had a Piano. We had pigs & a cow. The cow had to be tied in the pasture & I had to take her by a lead rope on a halter to the pasture. I will always remember the smell of that cow's breath – that's why I never liked the taste of milk. I don't remember how we got water in the kitchen, but the bathroom had a chemical toilet. Weekly baths were taken in large washtubs with heated water. We used the same water for all of us, I think.

Norman & Shelby were both born in that house on Middlebelt. It's odd, but it seems the memory was the same for both of them. I remember being next door at Skiver's & I remember looking thru the window & either Elvie or Opal holding up a baby to show us. I remember a birthday while we lived there & getting a real paper doll cutout book. I also remember a small bracelet too. I had a white rat while we lived there. It seems to me it was my pet – given to me by Jeff. Jeff was Kelly's brother. Somehow it got loose outside & evidently mated with the rats in the chicken coop, as Kelly found some black & white rats & there was a rat-shooting episode.

Mary Skiver was my age & lived next door. We played together all the time. There was a family named Lovasz. I believe they were Hungarian, with a son named Joe, who was Dwight's age. They were the first Catholic family I had ever known of. Also, there was a family named Hubbell – Their daughter, Caroline, was my age. She was a redhead. The whole neighborhood used to play together. I remember one time we were playing & one of the kids was jumping off the roof of an abandoned house & daring others to do the same. I jumped off the porch & turned at the same time, hitting my jaw on the porch. I bit my tongue all the way through, & went home, but was unable to say what happened. When my mom asked what happened, Dwight said I was doing the "dare" with the other kids & she thought I jumped off the roof. I couldn't explain what happened. I don't remember going to the doctor but I couldn't talk for a long time until it healed. For me, that was pretty bad, because I do like to talk. I remember playing baseball, too. One time I tried catching the ball without a glove & my fingers got bent. Also, when we lived on Middlebelt, Dwight worked for a family with goats. He worked to make money & gave it up to get a permanent for me.

One time we were home alone. We were making "hamburgers" out of pork sausage, with mustard, etc. I don't remember how it started, but we ended up throwing mustard at each other. When Mom came home it was a mess & he took the blame for the whole thing, & I let him. I don't know how much money Kelly made at the factory, but I guess he spent most of it on the "farming". Anyway, this one time, we were going to have new clothes for Easter – All ordered out of a catalog. I had a hat, dress, shoes, etc., & Dwight had a suit. They were all hanging on the door - we didn't have closets. This time we got into a fight - he took a slice at my dress, I took a slice at his suit, & we ended up really ruining those clothes. He again took the blame for it all. At that time, we heard at school that the Salvation Army was going to be at the airport to give out clothes for the people who needed, & I decided that since my dress was ruined, I'd go to the airport with them & get me some new clothes. We had to walk past our house to get from the school to the airport. Dwight ran home & told mom what I was doing, & she ran out & took me out of the line. She explained to me that it was for people who were really poor & we weren't that bad off. She had already ordered some new clothes for that Easter.

Lonnie & Nancy Filbeck's children were: Lois (married Burl Hubbs), Joseph L. (married Treva Threet) whose children were Dorothy Ann (Brooks). For some reason we always called her "Brooks", but her name was really Dorothy Ann. She married Herb Nichols & they had one child, Sherry. Sherry is about 3 yrs older than Patrick. When I lived with Aunt Lois, she played with him. Their next daughter was Laura June (married Bill), Joe Neal & then Barbara (married Jack). Don't remember some last names. The third was Trema Lillian (married Orvice Monroe Patton), children: Dwight Leroy, born on Jan 2, 1927(I think). Me, Nancy Jane, born April 9, 1932. They were divorced in 1935 & later (I think when I was about 5 or 6 yrs old, she married Kelly Barker. Norman Roger Barker was born on Feb 1, 1939. Shelby Joan was born a year after Norman on Jan 10, 1940.

Uncle Hoye Gilbert was the youngest son of Lonnie & Nancy. I remember when I did go to KY (Mom, Dwite & me), he was unmarried & still at home. He married Nellie & they had 2 sons: Gilbert Wayne (married Marion (Kay) King from Hillman). He lived in Detroit for a while & worked for Dwight. They moved to KY, had kids & she died a few years ago. Larry Richard married a girl who lived across the street from Aunt Lois, Sandy Blan. The youngest daughter of Lonnie & Nancy was Dixie (married Frank Fithian). He was a little short guy, and one of my favorites. Glenda Gayle married Ben Thompson & they live in KY. Joyce Elaine was the second (married someone, I don't remember his name). Sherry lives in Dearborn. Nancy Joan was the youngest – also named after Grandmother. One of those girls married a Mischloney & one married a Wenzel, I think, with relatives in this area.

On Dad's side, there was Fred (married Clara) & they had 2 daughters & one son who died in childbirth. Muriel Dene was about my age & Faye (Married Ed). Dene lives in Ohio & Faye lived next door to Uncle Fred. Aunt Marie (Verdon Tucker) had Jerry Don, Kay, & Jill. I never saw much of Jill. Uncle J.I. was the youngest. He didn't have a full name. They lived in Hazel, KY, near the KY, TN border. Their one daughter was named Nita Gayle. That year that I spent the summer in KY, Dene & I went to Uncle J.I.'s for a weekend & we had a good time teasing Nita Gayle. We told her that the way to get milk out of a cow was to pump the tail up & down so the milk would come out the faucets. We thought it was funny, but Uncle J.I. told us not to tease younger girls. Just recently I received an email with reference to country singer, Candy Coburn, who is Jill's daughter & who wrote & recorded a song about Aunt Marie, "Pink Ribbon Warrior".

Mom had a friend named "Sheelie" who would bring Dwite & I presents, & he also let mom use his car to take us down to KY. I have no idea what happened to him in later years. As I told you, I don't remember too much of when I was real little. We lived in what was known as Old Dearborn near the Ford Rouge Plant. Dwite probably has more memories of that time than I do. After we moved over on Middlebelt, I can remember a little more. We lived near the airport & had to move when they put the "Bomber Rd" in, which is now I 94. As I recall it, Dwight & Mom did most of the building & Kelly worked out near Ypsilanti. I remember listening to the radio as a family. I slept on the couch & I remember going to sleep to the sound of Inner Sanctum on the radio. We also listened to Jack Armstrong, the All-American Boy & other such programs. I particularly liked a program, 'I love a Mystery', which featured Jack, Doc, & Reggie as the stars. I think they were detectives. And, of course, "The Shadow Knows"...It was easy to imagine an invisible hero.

The Skivers lived next door. They had a daughter who was near my age – Mary. I have a picture of her that was sent much later (I think it is a graduation picture). Uriel & Opal Albright lived on the other side of us which I remember as being a white colonial. They had a piano & Opal played it very well, by ear. Junior Albright was about Dwight's age. Dwight worked for a goat farmer down the road & used his pay to pay for a permanent for me. At that time, the permanents consisted of solutions put on your hair, & then a big machine with a hood & curlers hanging down, which were attached to your head, and it seemed that the permanent was almost burned into the hair. I had very thick hair & usually before I got a permanent, my hair had to be thinned. They ran a comb through, which had a razor imbedded & it actually cut hair away.

Norman & Shelby were both born when we lived on Middlebelt. Norman had curly hair & was a very cute little boy – always getting into trouble. Shelby was a little "doll", & I would put her in my doll buggy & push her around. Once in a while Catherine & Herb would come to stay with us. They were Kelly's kids by his first wife, Kate. I think Catherine was a little older (about Dwight's age) & Herb was somewhere between Dwite & me. I remember not liking Catherine very much. She seemed to me to think she was better than us. We used to spend time on a "teeter-totter" made of a plank, on a saw-horse, & one time, when I was high in the air on one end, & she was on the bottom end, she just got off & let me go banging into the ground on my tail bone. Herb was another story – he was always getting into some kind of trouble, & I liked him a lot. One time he was mad & was going to leave home – Mom packed his suitcase & told him to go ahead. He ended up crying & staying. I never heard anything about Herb in later life. Catherine, on the other hand married a Ralph Kowalski, who had relatives in the UP. When we lived at Long Lake, they found out where we lived & came up to visit us. I then kept in touch somewhat until she died. She had a couple of beautiful daughters & I have a picture or two of them also at one of Shelby's kid's weddings.

Skivers had a big barn we used to play in. One time while Catherine & Herb were visiting us we were playing there & there was someone (probably Herb) threw a dart & barely missed putting Dwight's eye out. We used to put up a blanket like a tent & play house... sometimes mud pies, & sometimes we actually had beans to eat. At that time I thought God gave us babies & I remember Doris Skiver had a baby & she wasn't married. I couldn't figure that one out.

During the war, the airport became an army base & Gene Autry was there. I remember when Japan attacked Pearl Harbor, uncle Joe & Aunt Treva were visiting and when the news came over the radio, we all were listening & I remember Dorothy & Aunt Treva crying that they thought Uncle Joe would have to go into the army. I don't actually know of anyone who went into the army at that time, but there was a lot of activity at the airport & the big B27s were there...too big to fit in the hangar – they stuck out. There was a train viaduct that went over Middlebelt & we used to slide down the side hills on our sleds, sometimes going into the road. I remember the Baby Ruth candy bar, another called Whiz (the best nickel candy bar there is). They were only a nickel, and ice cream cones were 3 cents.

Kelly's family came from Tenn. I remember Bob & Elvie (don't remember last names) would come over & bring guitars & fiddles & play music. I think everyone came to our house on weekends. We never had a lot, but it seemed that Momma could make dinner for a crowd out of almost nothing. We ate a lot of pork chops, sausage, biscuits, potatoes, and beans at almost every meal. She used to bake cake & they always seemed to be heavy & soggy, not light & fluffy like now. Yellow cake with caramel frosting seemed to be the most common. Everything had to be canned or salted (cured) for keeping.

I went to Gordnier School. We walked country roads to get to school. One time I remember Herb cutting through the woods to get home & got his foot stuck in the railroad track. As I remember, it was just a 2-room school. I think 4th – 8th grade was in one room, & 1st thru 3rd in the other. There was some kind of food program. There were some kids who didn't even have shoes to wear. The food included raisins, nuts, or some form of dried fruit, etc. & it was distributed to us probably to make sure we had healthy food. We would stand up every morning, pledge allegiance to the flag & pray for God to bless our day.

I used to try to draw. I thought Aunt Dixie was quite an artist. She used to draw pictures for us & I tried to copy what she did. In the early days, I loved visiting with Aunt Dixie, but later, she became sick & finally bed-ridden & it was very hard to visit her because she never talked about anything anymore except how sick she was. Uncle Frank waited on her all the time. After Momma died & the summer after I turned 12, Aunt Dixie sat me down & told me the "facts of life". She told me about menstruation, but not in the way it is talked about now. She simply told me that one day I would start to bleed & would have to use padding to cover it up & that after that time, I would be able to have babies. I really didn't understand until I did start my periods & that was when I was 13. I was at school (Brace, next to Dad's), wearing a red & white dress & playing baseball with the kids at recess, when I noticed blood on my dress. I ran home & told Jay & she simply gave me a sanitary belt & pad & told me to put it on.

When we moved to VanBorn, I think it was because the State bought out all of the houses on Middlebelt to make way for the Bomber Rd. The VanBorn house had an actual coal furnace & a basement & a real bathroom with a bathtub & a toilet. It had a carpet & we had to take our shoes off when we went to visit before moving in. Later, the carpet came out & we had linoleum. Coming in the back door, you had to go up stairs to the house or down to the basement & there was a sand cellar below the stairway. We had a barn & we used to slide down the haystack. There was rose-covered fence all around the yard. The house was beautifully landscaped with peonies, evergreen trees & a stone walk & a big yard. Across the road there was a big farm house & Kelly rented land across the road for farming. Dingmans lived in that house & Jackie Dingman was my age. We used to play in the barn over there. One time, we were playing & at supper time, Momma called for me to come home. I didn't answer, but instead hid in the barn. Jackie went home & Dwight & Mom came looking for me. When we went home she asked if I didn't hear her calling my name. I said I hadn't heard. I remember her looking me in the eye & telling me I wasn't telling the truth. She said she was going to give me a spanking (& she did), not because I had stayed in the barn, but because I lied. She had clear green eyes, & I thought she could see right into my head.

I remember when we moved into the VanBorn house, things were being moved in trailers from the other house, & they unloaded stuff & let me stay there to put away fruit jars & light stuff while they went back for another load. It was summer & I got hot & thirsty. I went to get a drink of water. I thought I would be sick. The water was sulphur water & it tasted like rotten egg shells. Later on, I remember Jay putting eggshells in water to "feed" her plants, & it smelled awful, but that's what I think the water tasted like. I thought we really had a problem, since we were just moving into this beautiful new house & couldn't drink the water. Of course, I was wrong. The water was perfectly safe for drinking & once you got used to it, you didn't notice it – it tasted good & normal city water wasn't as good. It did take a while to get used to it.

Kelly had a brother named Jeff. His wife was Minnie. She helped me bake a cake & once when I finally baked a cake, with Minnie's help, that was lighter than what Mom baked, she told me I could bake all the cakes after that. One chore I hated was washing dishes! It was my job to clean the table after eating & wash the dishes. We had to use two large dishpans, set on the table & filled with heated water. One was for washing & the other for rinsing. Dishes weren't so bad but I hated the pans. They were greasy & too big to fit in the dishpans. Every chance I got, I would take all the pans & hide them in the oven & just wash the dishes, until I got caught. I never got spanked for it; in fact, I think Mom thought it was kind of cute. When Minnie taught me to bake a cake, she also taught me that when you use the pots & pans, it is your responsibility also to clean them. So, the lesson was finally learned – I couldn't hide them forever. She was my first experience with death. She had breast cancer & had a mastectomy. I remember thinking how odd she looked with one side of her breast being flat. She eventually died & that was the first funeral I ever remember going to. I don't remember what my feelings were at the time.

Since I'm talking about cleaning off the table, I'll relate this also. Coffee was a grownup drink. Kids weren't allowed to drink coffee. Well, if I couldn't do it, I certainly wanted to! So, when I cleared the table after eating, I would take the coffee cups, pour the leftover dregs into one cup & then I would drink the forbidden "coffee". You can imagine how that mixture of cold, stale coffee tasted – and that's the reason I don't drink coffee to this day.

Also about that period of time, I remember going to the grocery store. We didn't have super markets like we do now.

Small grocery stores, individually owned, kept all kinds of groceries. There was a long stick with a kind of hook on the end, used to get things like cereal boxes, etc. off the top shelves. They had barrels that held pickles, crackers, flour, etc., which was scooped out & purchased by the pound. Most of the time, we stayed in the car while Mom & Kelly went inside. One time we were waiting & this little fuzzy poodle-type dog came around. We took him in the car with us & decided we could keep him. When Mom & Kelly came out with the packages, which weren't many. We had most of our own vegetables, meat & such, so we only had to buy the staples, such as flour, cereal, etc. Sometimes we got a treat & they bought us some hard candy. I remember when oleo first came out, it was white like lard & there was a color capsule that you had to break & mix in it to make it look yellow. Anyway, they came out to the car & when we started home, Norman couldn't keep his mouth shut; he started telling them about this dog. As it turned out, it was a stray & we kept him. We called him Poodles. We used to sell tomatoes, corn & eggs along the side of the road. We set up a stand across the road from the house & Dwight & I would stand out there & when cars would stop by, we would sell to them. I think tomatoes were probably a nickel each, & we would sell eggs. When they wanted fresh corn, Dwight would go into the field & pick it fresh. Anyway, the dog used to come out there with us. I thought he was such a cute little guy. I'm not sure, but I think he got run over. We were allowed to keep the money for ourselves & used it for going to the show, or some other thing.

About going to the show, one time I had the money & wanted to go. But I could only go with someone else. Dwight used to hitchhike to go to the show, & this time Mom said I could go with him. He made me stay way back, because he said people wouldn't stop if they saw me. When someone would stop, I had to run up & get in the car too. We went to the

Wayne Theatre at that time. Dwight also got a job at that show as an Usher. He had a uniform with a vest with gold buttons & the neat pants with a sharp crease. I was so proud of him. Once we went to pick him up after work, & I walked in & the show was still on. The movie was Voyager & I got to watch a little of it. It was a romantic movie & usually I couldn't watch that kind of movie. I think Bette Davis & Paul Henried were in it. Not only was he in uniform, but he was my big brother – I thought he was so important & I was so proud.

One time after we were at the show, we found a little stray cat & we picked him up & took him home. He was very strange in that he didn't seem to eat anything. Once we took him along to Aunt Dixie's & she had corn on the cob & some fell on the floor & the cat ate it. It was the oddest thing – it seemed that the only thing that cat would eat was corn. He finally died – maybe from starvation, I don't know.

Aunt Dixie was an excellent cook. In fact, I think all my aunts were good cooks, except for Aunt Lois. Uncle Burl always did the cooking for her. Aunt Dixie had a pressure cooker. One Thanksgiving, I remember being at Aunt Dixie's & she had a turkey that was just buried in dressing in the roaster. At our house on VanBorn, the cousins & Aunts & Uncles used to come over on weekends. We had an ice cream maker. It was set in a tub with ice & some kind of coarse salt was poured all around it, & someone had to turn the crank. Aunt Lois brought along the black walnut flavor to go in with the cream, eggs & vanilla to make the ice cream. It was always a nice time. Eventually it would come around to someone playing the guitar.

I don't think any of my aunts & uncles ever drank; although I heard a story that Uncle Frank was once a drunk & was now sober. Mom & Kelly used to drink beer with Opal & Uriel Albright. Opal & Mom were best friends & I used to hide behind the couch & listen to them talking & laughing while they drank beer & smoked 20-Grand cigarettes. We had a radio-record player that looked something like a juke box. When Kelly would get drunk & Mom would get mad at him, he would end up bringing home some kind of present. I think the radio was one of them. It had colored glass & played stacked records. We had a piano on VanBorn also. It was a player piano & we had rolls that went in & would play automatically. Mom could play a little by ear, but not as well as Opal. She said she was going to get lessons for me as I got a little older. I did learn the scales & a very small part of "Are you washed in the Blood", a church song.

I went to Haiti school & there were a couple of blacks in the school. I thought I had a crush on one who seemed very nice. The riots broke out at Belle Isle at that time, & there were killings, etc., there. I couldn't understand what all the commotion was since we didn't have any problems with them at school. Once in a while I remember walking to school. I think I had 35 cents for lunch & I walked to a grocery store & bought cheese tidbits & hostess cupcakes for my lunch that day. I don't ever remember potato chips from that time. Cracker Jacks were a good snack. There was an after-school class where I learned to play the harmonica. I think Jeff may have bought me the harmonica. In the class we had to write down all the notes on paper & learn to play them. I actually learned to play "O, Suzanna" but I don't know if I could do it now. You put your fingers across certain holes so that when you puffed, those notes wouldn't sound.

We had chickens, a cow & a couple of horses I remember as Doc & Fanny. They were hooked up to plows, etc. & Dwight did most of the farm work. Sometimes we all got involved, like in tomato planting. I remember planting tomatoes. The rows had to be made, & I think, Kelly would make the furrow...Dwight would make the hole; Norman would drop a plant in each hole, and my job was to take one handful of cow manure from a bucket & put it in each hole with the tomato plant; I think Shelby & Mom may have been the ones who then covered it up. I hated that job, & probably hated Kelly more at that time than any other time in my life as I blamed him for it. Dwight remembers a lot more about the farming than I do. It wasn't a big farm, but enough to keep us busy. Dwight used to catch it from Kelly once in a while for not doing something just right.

Shelby was just a little girl who seemed to hate wearing clothes. There was a porch on the front of the house, & it was open underneath. She used to go underneath, take off her little dress & then come out to play with no clothes on. I remember having to catch her & dressing her again. Thinking on it now, Mom used to make most of our clothes, & Shelby wore little voile dresses & I think the seams must have scratched her. I can't imagine any other reason why she kept taking her dresses off. She was wearing one of those dresses when she got burned.

Shellidays lived next door to us & they had an adopted son about Norman's age. There was a homecoming in Wayne & Kelly had told us that we could go that evening, but only if the kids behaved. Norman was always getting into trouble & to make sure he was good, he didn't go outside to play. He was lying on the bed & watching them out the window. Mom was pregnant at the time & was dusting the piano, when Norm yelled & said Shelby was on fire. Mom ran out the front & by the time she got there, Mrs. Shelliday had grabbed a rug & had Shelby wrapped in it & in the car. Mom got in the car with her & they took off to Eloise hospital where both the Shellidays worked. I don't know for sure what happened, but Shelby was wearing one of those voile dresses & Skipper had struck a match & tossed it, landing on her dress, which went up in flames. She was probably 3 yrs old at the time. When they brought her from the hospital she had bandages all around her little body. Mom was pregnant so she couldn't handle the smell. Mrs. Shelliday taught me how to dress the wound. I used Ungentine to put on the wound & wrapped her in gauze. I remember the skin being black & the Ungentine made it smell even worse. She was lucky that the dress clung to her body & the flames didn't go up to her face. She still has a very bad scar around her body. Shellidays turned out to be very good friends & were a big help to us after Mom died. They had a big house, & the ceilings were decorated & looked like a big wedding cake. After Mom died, Mrs. Shelliday went to school with me for the Mother's Day program.

Our house on VanBorn had a full basement. Mom & Dwight put wallboard up & built a kind of little apartment down there. It was rented out. He also closed off the porch upstairs & that became his bedroom. The basement was rented by a lady named Marge, with a little girl about Shelby's age. The kids were kind of afraid of the coal cellar because it was so dark. Whenever they did something wrong, we told them Old Joe was going to get them – he was an imaginary man who lived in the coal cellar. When they began to disbelieve, Margie dressed up in an old hat & dirty clothes & pretended to be him.

In October of 1943, Opal was visiting & she & Mom were in the bathroom & something was wrong. Opal came out & gave me a package to take down & throw in the furnace. Being a curious kid, I looked inside & it was bloody stuff & I thought someone was going to die. Evidently, Mom had started bleeding & Kelly & Opal took her to the hospital & she had the baby. I don't know all the details, but the baby was born dead. Opal came & asked me to help find some clothes for the baby to be buried in. I went through the dresser & found a dress that mom had made. Opal said Mom had a tumor & that it had eaten away at the baby. She took the dress & she & Kelly buried the baby. It wasn't named, but I think it was a boy.

Mom came home & was home for Thanksgiving & did her Christmas shopping from the catalog. When she went back into the hospital in December to have the tumor removed, she told me that I could go above the closet & in the Christmas presents, there was a dress, which she had bought for me for Christmas. She said it was kind of grown-up & if I put it on, I would be able to visit her in the hospital because you had to be 13 to visit. I never got the chance. Dwight & Kelly went to visit her & Dwight said she told him to take care of us kids. I don't remember, but I guess Kelly was called back & when he came home, he put his hat on the dining room table & said "Your Maw's dead".

Everything during that time was very traumatic for me & I don't know that I remember everything correctly, but she was laid out in a casket in the living room, & chairs were set up in the dining room. The relatives were there, & I tried very hard to be good & understand what was happening, but I couldn't. I was learning to knit at the time & I took out my needles & yarn & started doing that to have something to do, & I was told to put it away as I had to respect my mother. I didn't know what that meant. I couldn't bring myself to touch that person in the casket. I just knew that my mother was gone, but that wasn't her. I don't remember crying. The day of the actual funeral, I was walking over to Mrs. Shelliday's with Dorothy Brooks to get my hair combed & curled & Dorothy asked me why I wasn't crying. She said "If my mother died, I would cry". I just remember saying, Mom wouldn't want me to. She'd want me to be brave. I think I felt guilty about not crying, but to me she just wasn't dead, but was still with me somehow. I never understood what I was supposed to do, except just to be there. Dad & Jay came & I overheard Aunt Dixie & Aunt Lois saying it was obvious that Orvice was still in love with Trema. I don't remember the funeral, but someone (maybe Elvie) sang "The Old Rugged Cross" because Aunt Lois said it was Mom's favorite song. I don't remember the cemetery or anything. Mom was born May 13, died on December 13, & there was something about her hospital room was 313 & the grave number has 13 in it & probably it is right next to the baby's grave.

When I was doing research on the computer, I obtained a copy of the death certificate & it says she died of a "coronary embolism" following a hysterectomy. When she went to the hospital she was to have surgery to have the tumor removed, & as I understand it, the surgery was successful, but she developed the blood clot after. A lot of years later, Shelby & I went to visit Opal & she told us that the tumor had been cancerous & that she would have died from that had she not died of the blood clot. She also told us that Kelly blamed the doctor & wouldn't pay his bill.

When she made plans to go into the hospital, she needed someone to take care of the kids as Dwight & I were both in school, and Shelby & Norman were not yet. Edith was 19 years old & she and her sister had been living with Aunt Lois. She came over to take care of the kids & do the housework while Momma was in the hospital. Afterward, she stayed on. She slept with Shelby & me in my bedroom. It didn't take too long, & I don't remember just how everything happened, but Edith would get up during the night & go into Kelly's bedroom. At any rate, she got pregnant, although I didn't know it. But I used to argue with her & this one day I was really mad at her & told her she couldn't tell me what to do because she wasn't my mother & she said pretty soon she would be running the house & I would have to mind her. Dwight was out in the yard & I went out to complain to him. He said there wasn't anything to worry about because he had contacted Dad & he was coming to pick me up. He said he would come later after he finished up his school year. He said that Edith & Kelly were getting married. I was sad to be leaving Norman & Shelby, but felt kind of smug about the idea, that I wasn't going to have to listen to Edith. So, that was when we moved over to live with Dad & Jay. This was the summer that I was 12. I went to the 7th & 8th grades at Brace School.

Dolores was Jay's daughter, a little older than Dwight. She was kind of weird but she & I shared a bedroom. After Dwight was old enough to get a driver's license & had a car, we would go back to visit Norman & Shelby on Sundays, birthdays, & holidays every chance we got. On the way over, or coming back, we would stop at a restaurant & I remember having veal cutlets. I really felt grownup to be eating out.

Dwight went to Redford High, but he quit school & joined the Navy. I graduated from the 8th grade at Brace. Jay never liked me very much; maybe she was afraid that Dad would do more for me than for Dolores. I really don't know why, but she would yell at me every chance she got. I really didn't care that much because I didn't really like her either & I thought Dolores was just plain dumb. I never talked much to my Dad either. He seemed to be either at work or busy all the time.

Then when one of Dwight's friends, Larry Johnson, was getting married, we went to the wedding & were having a really good time. Someone started the crazy deal of cutting off ties, & when they went to cut off Dwight's he reached up & got his hand cut. I think they took him to the hospital or something, at any rate I was quite concerned about him. This was after he had come home from the Navy & had moved out of the house. The next day, I called to see how he was &

Jay caught me & got mad because I was using the telephone without asking her. She started yelling at me & telling me I was "dragged" up. Later, I don't know if Dwight told him, or if Dad just came home to it; but anyway, he came home from the bar & told me to get my coat & get in the car with him. We went to a restaurant in Redford & this was the first time I had ever talked to him about anything. When I was in high school & needed anything, I would just go to Dwight. Anyway, this time, he asked me to tell him what the problem was. I was crying & I told him I didn't care what she said about me, but that I wasn't going to let her criticize my mother. He told me I should never let anyone criticize my mother – she was the only woman he ever loved. After that, I felt a little closer to him, but it wasn't too long after that Dwight got married to Janie & I moved in with them after they moved to the corner of Plainfield & Acacia.

The Wilkinsons lived across the street from Dad & they had a big family. June was my age & we were best friends. I would go back to the neighborhood & visit with the Wilkinsons. Dolores Wilkinson worked with Dick Green in a little shop on 8 Mile Rd., & he also spent time at the Wilkinsons. I originally met him at a party at O'Dea's where he came with his brother Norvel. I remember thinking Norvel was cute, but too young. I didn't find out that Dick was only a month older than me until later when we got our marriage license. Anyway, one time we were all at the Wilkinsons & just sitting around talking. I wrote the days of the week on slips of paper & put them in the middle of the table & told the guys, to pick their days. There was Frank Wilkinson, Jack Spencer, Marvin Wilkinson, Bob Spencer, Russ Duffy, Dick Green & a couple of others. They all picked a day & we laughed about our "dates". I was quite surprised when Dick actually came over to Dwight's on the day he had picked. After that, we saw each other occasionally at Wilkinsons & even went to the show one time with Bob

Westermeier. When Dwight & Jane moved to the house on Westover, it was directly behind Brunings where Dick was living, & he ended up coming over almost every evening. Actually, Russ Duffy also came over on his day, but he just wanted to talk about Pat Johnson.

Dick never felt that his family loved him. From what he had told me I remember thinking that his mother was a very rich woman & I had her pictured as being very slim, good looking, artsy & ritzy-looking. He told me that he was born before his mother & dad married, and from the way he talked, I imagined them as kind of above everyone else. I guess he felt he wasn't really wanted as he lived with his grandparents & his parents never took him to live with them. I understand that they did take him for a while when they lived in Moltke but I don't know a whole lot about it. After we were married Aunt Doris & Grandpa & Grandma Green told me a little about the family. I don't know that much, but Esther was the oldest daughter of Bill & Freida Green. She had one sister, Doris & a brother, Arnold. She dated Stanley Koss. His father was Tony. I never met or knew his mother, but I think she was Woloszyk. I'll get into their families later. I did some computer research on them also.

After we moved over with Dad on Evergreen in Southfield, I adjusted to living with a stepmother & a stepsister. Jay (her name was Julia Ann, but most people called her Jay) resented me & I later realized that she was afraid that Dad might give me preference over Dolores; although, he never even talked to me most of the time. Dolores was 5 years older than me, but it didn't take long to realize that she was not very smart. She had difficulty in school & when she was a freshman at Redford High; Jay was called in & told that she needed special attention. She was put in an all girl school, but that didn't last too long. Whenever I wanted to go somewhere – the show, or just for a walk – I had to take Dolores with me. She had no friends of her own. She spent many summer days sitting on the big rock at the corner of the driveway & she would wave to guys driving by.

One time the two of us went to Edgewater Park (it wasn't far from our house); and when we got off the Ferris wheel, there were a couple of guys who wanted to pick us up. She wasn't cute or even pretty, but there was something about her that attracted the wrong guys. I decided I wanted to go home instead; so she went with them & I went home. She had the key to the house, so when I got there I managed to open the bathroom window & crawl in. I left footprints in the bathtub & the next morning, Jay woke us up & asked about the footprints in the bathtub. I said it was me that I had come home separately & didn't have the key. When she asked why, I told her to ask Dolores. Dolores told her she had met up with a couple of old school friends who wanted to go for ice cream & I refused to go. Needless to say, I not only had to clean up the bathtub, but got grounded. Dolores got pregnant. That was the night she met Loren Prosser, Patty Ann's father. He did come over & date her after that, & when the family found out she was pregnant, there was a big meeting that ended up with Dad taking them to Ohio or Indiana & he paid to have a marriage certificate back dated. In those days, it was a disgrace to have a child out of wedlock.

They lived with his parents for a while; then got a small apartment on their own. Jay would cook meals & take to them. That didn't last either, & they divorced soon after Patty was born & Patty was raised by Jay as her own. Dolores never learned how to take care of her. I'm not going to dwell on this, but she never did learn. She married her second husband Ken (I think) Wambles & had 3 kids with him before he left her & she came back to Dad's to live. Greg, her youngest, was Dad's hope. He did everything he could do for him & hoped that he would turn out great, but he didn't.

I went to Brace school which was next door to Dad's on Evergreen. I played softball & had lots of friends. In the eighth grade, we started a Brace Newsletter. I was the editor & we put it together on a ditto machine. I still have a copy but it is almost completely faded out. I also won the school spelling bee & received a Webster's Dictionary with my name engraved on it. I went on to the District Bee & won a pin & certificate which I still have. I didn't have any problem getting good grades in school – I think because back on VanBorn I remember that Mom used to help us with homework & she would have Dwight & I spell words together & also drilled us with multiplication tables. I think she would have been a great teacher.

Getting back to my high school days, I started out thinking I would go to college, then decided not to & took some business courses. Later found that in order to get honors for graduation, I had to have certain "college" courses. I had good enough marks for it, but needed a couple of different classes. I had a full slate of business courses & had to get parental permission to take on extra courses, & Dwight signed the papers for me. I graduated from Cooley with a Cum Laude Certificate. I could take shorthand at 140 words per minute & knew bookkeeping, but I didn't know what I wanted to do. I wanted a career. Dad offered to get me a job at Ford's but I didn't want to be dependant on anyone. I wanted to do it myself.

At one time I thought I would like to own a big house with lots of room & have a boarding house for working women. I gave that up & thought I would be an airline hostess, but it turned out I was too tall. Then I thought I might join the Waves (Pat Johnson's sister, Winona, was a Wave). When I graduated, the thing to do was to get a job. At that time, you wore a hat & gloves, suit, etc. when looking for office work. I put my application in all over Detroit. One day June & I started walking to 8 Mile where we would get a bus to go downtown. Jay came after me & told me I had a phone call. It was the Detroit Board of Education who said they had a job offer if I was interested. I went downtown, stood in line until my turn. When I finally reached the desk, the gal there had a very large book which she opened to a marked spot. This was before computers & this was a very large book of high school graduates. She had my name marked & my grades & qualifications. She referred me to Kerr Manufacturing.

I went in & got a job as Secretary to the Sales Manager. I started out making $85 a week. I had to take a couple of buses to get there. It was a dental manufacturing company on 12th street. My boss was Harry Lange, Sales Manager with 14 Salesmen. It was a very interesting job. I worked with a couple of gals, Marcy & Betty. Marcy worked in accounting & Betty worked in bookkeeping. We used to go downtown after work sometimes & at that time Detroit was less dangerous than now. One time walking across Woodward Avenue we stopped, and started pointing upwards, talking & oohing & aawing until everyone stopped & starting looking. We then just walked away, leaving everyone trying to see what we had seen. At the time it was very funny, & harmless. At one time, the 3 of us decided we would join the military. We went downtown to the Federal Building & picked up a bunch of papers & got locked in the building. I don't remember now how we got out – had to find a janitor or something.

One of my very first vacation trips was when we 3 decided to take a trip to New York City. We made arrangements to fly out of Detroit. Our NY salesman got us tickets to a show starring Nannette Fabre. It was a very exciting thing for 3 girls 18 years old on their own in New York City. We wore hats, gloves, dressing up to the "tee". We flew on a DC 7. At that time it was a lot smaller airport. We had to walk to the airplane. I had a navy blue suit, a red white-dotted hat. We were the only females on the plane except for the stewardess. When we got to the NY area, we ran into some storm. I was laughing because Betty was sick & nauseous, but then I had to grab the bag because I had to throw up. They then announced that we couldn't get into LaGuardia because of the weather; but instead would be landing in Philadelphia. A couple of salesmen helped us get our bags, etc., & we took a train from Philadelphia to Grand Central in New York. This only added to our experience. We checked into our hotel room & had a grand time. I don't remember how many days we had, but we walked around Times Square, went to the Statue of Liberty, the brand new (still unoccupied) UN building, picked up a couple of Marines & a Sailor in Central Park, & all in all had a wonderful time. We weren't old enough to go into a bar, but we did other things. We went to Rockefeller Plaza & saw a TV show being taped – I think it was The Hit Parade. We went shopping on 5th Avenue. I bought a dress & had it mailed home. We watched as pizza was tossed by a baker in a shop window. At that time, we had never eaten or even seen a pizza.

Another time we took the train from Detroit to Ann Arbor & went to U of M to see a football game. The first time I had ever seen a football game. I never went to one in high school. I took swimming, field hockey, basketball, fencing, but never joined any groups, so the football game was new to me. I think they played Indiana & we had a great time on the train, as well as at the game. We decided we were going to go to California; but that kind of fell through when I met Dick & decided to get married.

The day that Dick & I decided to get married, we went to Lord's in Redford & picked out my engagement ring; then came home (I lived with Dwight) & Dwight had a phone call saying Grandmother Patton was very ill. He was going to Kentucky & wanted me to go with him. I didn't want to leave Dick, but Dwight said, bring him along. So we all went down there together. I think Grandmother Patton was in the hospital & we did go to visit her & we visited with Grandmother & Granddad Filbeck. When we came back we started talking about getting married. I had always thought April was a nice time to get married, but he said, no, he wanted to get married some other time. He had been engaged to another girl (Millie Gimmel) and they had planned on getting married in April; & had broke up when Norvel told him she was dating other guys while he was working in Detroit. That's how we decided to get married in February instead. I also remember one time when Norvel took me aside & told me if I thought I was going to marry his brother, I had another think coming. I think he later changed his mind, though. We made plans to go up North & meet his family, and since I didn't really go to church that much we were going to get married in his church in Posen. He had a 1941 Ford and we went up North to meet his family.

Back then there was no I-75 & we drove out Telegraph, went thru Waterford, and on M-15 somehow to US 23. The drive would take about 7 hrs. no matter how you went. We stayed with Grandma & Grandpa Green. They were very nice. Arnie & Stella lived with them. Esther & Stanley lived in the old farmhouse...directly behind the Green farm acreage. It was a tall house with artificial red brick siding. The kitchen was rather large, a dining room & again a small room which eventually was made into a bathroom, but at that time, there was a pump in the kitchen & an outhouse. The living room was usually closed off & used only for special occasions. It wasn't until TV came in that people began to use the living rooms.

Most activities took place in the kitchen. I learned how to play Spitzer & we also played Pinochle. Everyone played a lot of cards to pass the time.

I was very surprised when I met Esther. I had thought she was a really classy lady from what Dick had told me. I had already met Norvel; Janet was very young, & Edna & Earl were almost like twins. They were always together. There was snow & it was cold, but it was a very nice visit & I liked the area & all of the people I met. Grandma Green told me about Dick's previous engagement shower. In those days, the shower was like a reception, with everyone invited & music & a big dinner. Since the shower had taken place there, the gifts were still at Grandma's house. She showed me all of the things & gave them to me; they were mostly linens, etc. There also was an engagement ring. I didn't want it, and have no idea of whatever happened to it.

I met a lot of the guys Dick had hung around with in Posen. We went to Hillman to pick up a couple of girls for Doc Schellie & Gerry Misiak, and we went to the Avalon bar. Although we still weren't old enough to drink the guys were all drinking beer. Mostly, we just danced to the juke box. I liked most everyone I met & I really liked Grandma & Grandpa Green. We went to Hawks to meet with the pastor, Rev. Otto Koenig & his wife. He shared the two churches. We made most of the arrangements for the wedding on that trip. Another guy, a friend of Dick's, was Lenny Soik. His girlfriend (who later became his wife) had the last name of Patin. At that time I didn't meet too many of the girls who later became our circle of friends, but all the guys were the same.

When we came up for the actual wedding, Dwight & Jane had a green Dodge car & Roger sat in the back with one of his buddies to help hold the wedding cake I had bought in Redford because Dick had told me there weren't any bakeries in Posen. We had ordered our flowers from Linke's in Alpena, & had made arrangements for a photographer in Alpena. We had to drive to Alpena after the wedding to have studio pictures taken. Pictures at the church & reception were taken by friends with their own cameras. I borrowed my wedding dress from Dolores Wilkinson, and Pat Johnson & June Wilkinson wore blue bridesmaid gowns from Dolores' wedding. Even my shoes were borrowed. Bob Spencer had a new Ford & he drove up with June. Dick & I rode up with Russ Duffy & Pat Johnson. Pat & June stayed with me at Grandma Green's & Bob & Russ stayed at the Fletcher Motel in Alpena.

Needless to say, the old farmhouse was kind of crowded & my temper was kind of short. There was a wood stove in the kitchen at that time. Arnie & Stella were in the bedroom off the kitchen, Grandma & Grandpa Green were in the front bedroom, June & Pat were in the other bedroom, I was on the couch in the living room, & Dick was in the little room that later became the bathroom but at that time had a small single bed in it. There was a pump in the kitchen and an outdoor john. Stella & Grandma Green were baking pies for the wedding reception on the wood stove in the kitchen & the dining room table was set up for the next day. I remember Dick teasing about something as I was taking a pie out of the oven & I dropped it. I was very angry, but Pat said something to Dick & I took it out on her instead! I had to apologize to her later. It was a very hectic evening before the wedding day, and the morning didn't go much better.

Dick had arranged for Clarence Purol & his band to come to the house & play for us to leave for the church. Evidently, it was some kind of tradition there. I think it just added to the frustration, what with all those people trying to get dressed & ready for the wedding! The Koss's came to the house too & Reuben & Doris & Roger & Gerry & Penny, who was just a baby. I think they all came for breakfast. Reuben was going to stay home with Penny because she was cranky, and Stanley & Esther said they were going to stay at the house, too. They didn't want to go to the wedding because it was in the Lutheran Church. Reuben convinced them to go, and I remember, they stood at the back during the ceremony. I don't know where Dad & Jay, Dwight & Jane & the rest stayed, but some of the Wilkinsons who came stayed at Jerry's cabins in Posen & generally had a ball!

The reception was held in Posen at the C of C hall & Clarence Purol's band played the music. I learned to do the Polka at my wedding. I talked to Irv & Viola Reisner, who later became good friends & to Lori Lewandowski & other Wozniaks & generally had a pretty good time myself. We stayed at the hall until we closed it down; then went back to the farm. I had been expecting that we would go to a motel for our wedding night, but instead ended up at the farm. We sat at the dining table opening gift cards until very late, and we spent our wedding night in the little room that eventually became our bathroom! Quite a start! The next day June, Pat, Bob & Russ returned to Southfield. Dick had developed quite a cold, even before the wedding – it shows on our wedding picture, his glands were quite swollen. He was sick most of the week we spent there before coming back. He had received his draft notice, and Grandpa Green went with him to the draft board & convinced them that he needed Dick to help him with the farm & got a deferment. So, with that, he had to stay on the farm. I came home & made plans to quit my job, so I could move up to Posen. I had originally planned on us living in Farmington, but that didn't work out at all.

I gave notice at work & trained a replacement and finally made arrangements to move to Posen in April. Dwight & Jane agreed to drive me up. Dick went to Alpena (there were no phones in Posen) and called the day we were to leave & said we needed to stay on US 23 from Alpena since there was a snowstorm coming. It was raining in Southfield, so we didn't think it would be much of a problem. I had all my things packed in that old green Dodge, and we started out. Not too far out of Standish, it started snowing pretty heavily. By the time we got North of Alpena, we were barely crawling through the snow. We made the turn on M-65 from US-23 and managed to get about halfway to Posen when we just couldn't go any further. We were stuck right in the middle of the road. Dwight got out & walked to a farmhouse (Binga's) & borrowed a shovel. As he was digging out, the Momrik boys came by (John & Frank) & helped to get us out. We managed to get into Posen & at Vince's garage we found that a couple of the County drivers were waiting for Ermie Blemke to get a plow out of the County garage & come in to get them. So, we went into Jerry's Café & I unloaded my stuff & Jerry let me stay in his cabin. Dwight gassed up the car, turned around & started back to Southfield, leaving me there.

I was pretty lonely & confused, but happy that the locals had befriended me. I had no idea of how long I would be stuck there. The plows finally did get through the main road & Norvel & some of his buddies came into Posen. Jerry hailed him down & told him I was in the cabin, so he came & got me & my stuff & took me to Koss's, & he trudged through the snow to the farm to tell Dick I was there. They got the tractor out & plowed the road so I could get to the farm. I don't think I saw a worse storm after that time; or maybe it just seemed that way because we didn't have any of the phones, plows, etc. that we did later. Anyway, that was my move to Posen. The next day was Palm Sunday, April 2, 1952.

Dick was working on the farm & we stayed there for quite a while. Arnie was working out as a carpenter. I was anxious to get a job & Grandpa Green would take me to Alpena at least once a week to go to the unemployment office & look. I decided that I had to learn to drive so that I could drive to Alpena myself. I thought it was like in Detroit that you had to learn & then get a permit. I kept nagging at Dick to take me to get a permit. Sheriff Sorgenfrei gave me a written test & I got all the questions right. Then there was to be a driver's test. He was busy & didn't have a lot of time. He asked if I could "snake in" & I just looked at Dick, & he said, sure. So, the Sheriff gave me a license & I didn't even know how to drive. Grandpa had an old green car at the time & he let me drive it around until I learned. It then got so I was driving his car & taking him wherever he wanted to go. At that time, Farmers were not included in the Social Security program & the Farm Bureau was holding meetings to familiarize the farmers with filing income tax. I went with Grandpa to all of the meetings & ended up helping most of the local farmers fill out their required income taxes so they could begin to collect Social Security.

Finally, I got a job at Montgomery Ward's – they said it would eventually be an office job, but started in sales. I worked in the basement, selling house wares, dishes, utensils, etc. for $75 per week, plus commission on everything I sold over $400 a week. I think I averaged around $75 to $80 those first weeks. I kept searching for office work & in August of that year, I went to work at Thunder Bay Manufacturing. I used to drive into work with some other girls that worked in Alpena. There was Martha Kuznicki (later married Alex Krajniak) who lived on a farm across the road, & a Nancy (later married Ray Koss) from around Bolton, Esther Koss & a couple of other gals who worked at McClellans dollar store.

That old 41 Ford did well, but the speedometer didn't work & not having driven before, I really had no idea of how fast I was driving. One time I had filled up with gas in Alpena at the Shell Station in town then left everyone off down the French Rd, & when Martha & I were the only ones left, I noticed something funny. I smelled gas & I stopped at the corner of Long Lake Rd & got out, but couldn't see anything. I told Martha I thought I was running out of gas & she said we should get someplace before we did. So, I started driving faster, trying to get to the little store called Dun Roamin that Charlie DeFrance owned. I finally got up to the store, slammed on the brakes, left some marks on the road & wheeled in. Charlie came running out to see what was wrong. I told him I thought I was running out of gas. He took a look & saw that the gas tank was hanging down & every time I went around a curve I was pouring gas out. He laughed, but he did manage to tie the tank up to stop it. I made him promise not to tell Dick. I don't know if he ever did; but I finally confessed.

There was another time when I was taking Martha home; if you remember on the old Kuznicki farm there was a gate at the end of the driveway. We would have to stop – Martha would get out & open the gate while I drove through, then close the gate & get back in & I would have to do the same when I drove out. They had cattle grazing & the gate had to be kept closed to keep them in. Once I was talking & not paying a lot of attention & drove right through the gate & broke a piece off the grill & bent the front fender. We managed to get the gate back up; & I made Martha promise not to say anything. When I got home, I pulled the car up around the side, on the hill & parked as I usually did. Dick always came out & kind of inspected his car & this time when he did, he came in the house & said "What in hell did you hit with the car?" I told him I didn't know that I hadn't seen anything wrong. He said the left fender is banged up & a piece of the grill was gone. He knew I used to nose in to the parking lot next to the foundry near the A & P. I told him I had parked as usual. He tried to figure it out & finally decided that I had pulled in on an angle & if another car pulled up next to me on an angle, it could have happened. He finally was satisfied & it was some time before I told him what had actually happened. I left Ward's to go to work for Thunder Bay Manufacturing. I worked as a Secretary to Francis Owen and my salary was $80 per week.

At that time, Thunder Bay Manufacturing and Alpena Supply were combined companies working out of the same office building & owned by Francis Tait & Walter Schmitt. They decided to split the two companies and Francis took on Thunder Bay. Gladys Wysocki, Chris Millsom, Thelma Bowen, Jean Guy & I worked together at Thunder Bay. Gladys was favored by Francis Owen & when it was necessary to cut back she was asked which job she wanted, & who she wanted to work with. She decided Jean should be laid off (although I had been the last one hired) & I was then given the payroll job. I got angry about it & said some nasty things to Gladys. Sometime later I decided that I had been too harsh with Gladys & made an attempt to apologize to her. She put her arms around my shoulder & said "That's ok, Nancy, we all have our bad days!" – And, I got mad all over again. I don't think she ever understood that she hadn't been fair to Jean.

Jean & Allen Guy became good friends of ours. Jean was just a little older than me & we would go out on weekends & she could drink. When I turned 21, Alice Paul decided I should learn to drink. Dick worked with Harry Paul at that time grading potatoes. They always ended up at the bar drinking. Alice came to pick me up & we started in Posen, went on to the Flying Duck, and probably every other bar in the vicinity until we found Dick & Harry. It was smelt season, and we went out somewhere netting smelt. I was drinking sloe gin & seven up, which was a very sweet drink, & my first preference. I drank enough that I got sick & ended up on the floor of the back seat – head hanging out, puking pink! I didn't drink that again.

At Jerry Bruning's wedding to Emmet St. Onge, I was helping out behind the bar & was mixing gin & squirt – heavy on the gin & short on the squirt. Reuben took me outside (it was at the Alpena Armory) for fresh air, but it didn't help much! I got really loaded & the next day, spent it sitting on a stone pile, trying to sober up.

There was another time with Alex & Martha Krajniak when I drank Pina Colada until I got smashed. And, another with Rum & Coke. Eventually, I think I tried them all & ended up having too much of everything & stopped drinking altogether. I actually had more fun when I didn't drink. I could dance & enjoy myself & still feel good the next day!

Shelby & I went to Dwight's 70th birthday party & I couldn't think of a thing to give him. He has been more than a brother to me all my life – so, I wrote him a poem.

Ode to the 1st 20 yrs. Of Dwite Leroy

Orvice & Trema sure felt lucky
That cool winter day in Kentucky.
He was a gift from heaven,
That Baby Boy born in '27.....

"Orvice", "Willard", "Oetis", or "Lonnie",
Those names just seemed too funny.
Somehow, it just seemed right
To name that boy.....Dwite!

For more, they couldn't wish again,
Took that boy & moved to Michigan.
Five years, I suppose he spent dribbling,
And waiting for his new sister sibling!

Twas the end of childhood tranquility,
Now, he took on this new responsibility.
It was me he always took care of,
But all that, no one was aware of.

With funds so low & little means...
We grew up on beans, beans & more beans.
And there were names like Shiele, & Ocus.
Memories are there, but out of focus!

Kelly Barker joined the throng,
& we moved to Middlebelt 'ere long.
A house, built by Mom & Dwite..
Red brick shingles, & not white.

The family instantly grew.
Catherine & Herbie, the other two.
Also, animals, like pigs & chickens;
A cow, too, & vegetables for pickin'...

'39 & '40 were both big years,
for with them came two new dears.
Norman & Shelby, one after the other,
And more responsibility for big brother.

He watched us all with careful eye,
And wiped our tears when we did cry.
The best of brothers was our joy...
This gangly teen... Dwite Leroy!

The war broke out in forty-one
& our life on Middlebelt was done.
A beautiful house & five acres
On VanBorn – we're movers & shakers.

A couple of horses, Doc & Fanny
The memories there are many
My first trip to the show.
He stuck out his thumb & said "Let's go".

He got a job as a theatre usher.
No job I could imagine was plusher.
A uniform, cap and flashlight.
I was so proud of my brother, Dwite!

We sold corn & tomatoes at roadside.
A dog named Poodles was our joy & pride.
Eggs & vegetables, great for selling....
But the planting included a lot of smelling.

The manure, by hand, I put in the hole,
& the sun & heat took its toll.
While he sang "Ain't she sweet",
I still thought he was just so neat!

Sad days came when I was eleven,
Our Mom left & went on to Heaven.
And in charge, now, for sure,
Was our big brother; he did endure.

Though sad he was, and still in high school,
He took control & kept his cool.
He made decisions like a grown man,
And no one else could be greater than.

Though we two left & moved away,
With Norm & Shelby our hearts did stay.
He went to work and bought a car,
So we could visit – It was so far!

He joined the Navy & we were alone...
Just waiting for him to come home.
Then, one night I'll remember long,
He was home again & all fears were gone.

This first 20 years or so,
Is as far as I can go.
But, he was just as nifty,
Throughout the next fifty.

He was there through thick & thin.
A brother, father, and friend.
He's handsome; he's smart, & our joy...
This man, Pat...Brother, Dwite Leroy!

Nothing fancy, just a poem from your sister, Nancy.
January 2, 1998

My cousin, Dorothy (Brooks) died in 1995. We were both born in l932. She & I were pre-teens together. She was the one I talked to when Mom died. I used to spend weekends & overnights at her house. We both smoked, although she was a much heavier smoker than I. One time in high school, she passed out & when Uncle Joe took her to the hospital he was told that she was starving herself. She was naturally thin, but was always fearful of becoming fat (Like Aunt Lois). He was devastated & told her she had to eat. She died of lung cancer. We double dated a couple of times. She used to fix me up with guys. I used to tell her that all of her male friends were "greasy" looking. She married Herb Nichols. He was a very nice guy & doted on her. Dorothy always wanted to be a "somebody" & she was a real somebody to her family & friends. She wasn't the first of the cousins to die; in fact, her sister Laura June died of cancer a few years before. They were two completely different people. Aunt Treva had a rough time. It is very difficult to outlive your children. When Dorothy was sick I put a CB in my little blue caddy & drove down to KY to visit the relatives. It must have been the Christmas of 1989 or 90 because the car was an '89. I went on to Texas & Florida. I think it was the weekend before Christmas when I reached Aunt Treva's house. We went on to Dorothy's & to Barb's for an early Christmas. Dorothy & I enjoyed some good conversations & remembrances.

Uncle Joe was my mother's brother. He died a number of years before, & I went down to KY for the funeral, I think with Shelby & Norman. I understand Barb bought the farm & Aunt Treva was living with her. I recently learned that Joe Neal is the only one in that family still living. I know I'm at an age when my friends & relatives are going to be dying. I hope I don't outlive any of my children.

During the winter trip to KY, Texas & Florida I had some very interesting experiences. When I arrived at Aunt Treva's, she was fixing things to be taken to Barb's for the pre-Christmas dinner. She was making fried pies. I was so surprised, as my Mother was the only person I ever knew to make fried pies. Aunt Treva explained that it was my Mother's recipe. She made pie crusts, rolled them out & mixed up dried apricots, presoaked & put them on the crust, folded it in half & proceeded to fry them.

My next visit was to Uncle Fred's. I hadn't told them I was coming, but it was almost like they were expecting me. Aunt Clara had just taken a burnt sugar pie out of the oven.

Uncle J.I. & Aunt Louise were there visiting & I enjoyed some conversations & a piece of that burnt sugar pie. I told Aunt Clara that it was my favorite pie & she told me it was my mother's recipe. It is made by putting sugar in a cast iron frying pan & literally burning it to a caramel texture before adding the rest of the ingredients. It is finished by pouring into a pie crust, covering with meringue & toasting in the oven until the meringue is golden. I told them I was going on to Aunt Marie's before leaving for Texas for Christmas. Aunt Clara gave me the rest of the pie to take with me.

I then drove on to Almo where I stayed the night with Aunt Marie. I hadn't known it before, but she painted, very similar pictures, to the ones I had been painting. She worked in oils & had everything set up in a separate room. We really did enjoy talking about painting, etc., and old times. When I was ready to leave the next morning, she brought out a package of peanut butter fudge just the same as Grandmother Patton used to do when we were leaving after a visit. I then drove on down to Texas where I spent Christmas with Scott & his family.

That turned out to be another 'déjà' vou.... I was at Pat & Roger's she was preparing the turkey & it turned out just like Aunt Dixie's with the turkey buried in the dressing. I learned that the way to do that was to par-boil the turkey in a big kettle, making the juice for soup, dressing, etc., and then after stuffing the turkey, putting it in the roaster surrounded by more dressing & baking it just long enough to brown it, & since it was already almost cooked, it wasn't in the oven long enough for the stuffing to dry out!

After Texas, I drove over to Florida & stopped overnight at my cousin, Dene's place & got re-acquainted there too. Then I went on down & visited with my friends, Al & Grace

MacLennan. That's when I got hooked on soap operas. Grace taped the soaps while we went golfing in the afternoon, & then in the evening while we were playing cards, we watched the soaps. I still tape them everyday & watch when I have the time in the evening or on Saturday's; sometimes, watching a whole week of soaps at one sitting.

Another trip to KY would have been when Grandmother Filbeck died. I think that time I went down with Norman – another instance of southern hospitality & food. Neighbors had brought food over to Uncle Joe's after the funeral & there was a butterscotch pie that I've never forgotten & have been unsuccessful in duplicating. It was clear, similar to a lemon pie, but tasted very much like butter-rum life savers. The Filbeck Funeral Home, in Hardin, I believe, took care of the arrangements & the lady funeral director was enamored with Norman. She kept coming over & telling him what beautiful eyes he had. I had been unable to make it to KY for Granddad's funeral & this was my first experience. After the church service, the family was taken to a separate room & we were there to witness the closing of the casket. I remember Dorothy & I both discussing how she was being buried with her rings. I don't know if either one of us really wanted them, but it seemed that it would have been something to carry on as a family tradition. At any rate, we never said anything to anyone else. I came home with a quilt she had made & will treasure it always. I hope it will be treasured also by one of my granddaughters.

My cousin, Larry, died in 1996 & I went down to Detroit for his funeral. His only brother, Wayne was unable to make it to the funeral; but I was able to visit with other members of the family. Sherry Mischloney (Fithian) welcomed me into her home in Dearborn & we had a very nice visit remembering the 'good old days'. She was closer to Shelby's age, so I had not known much of her as a little girl. Later - I'm not sure how much later, managed to get all of the gal cousins together in Dearborn. Nancy, Joyce, Sherry & Glenda were all at home, & Shelby & me, along with Larry's widow, Sandy.

Once we moved to Posen, we didn't get the chance to go back to the Detroit area very often; mostly weddings & funerals. There were times when relatives or friends came up to visit with us. The first year we lived with Grandma & Grandpa Green since Grandpa had said he needed Dick to help him on the farm. When I went to work it helped us to have some money to do things on our own. After a while, Dick went to work at the foundry. We never had a lot of privacy & I really wanted to move out on our own, but we couldn't afford to pay rent on my salary alone. I began to have some problems with my periods & went to see Dr. Spens in Alpena. After examining me, he told me I was pregnant. I was very happy & began making plans to quit work & stay home with my new baby. I gained a little weight & even borrowed a maternity dress to wear to Earl's Christmas party at the schoolhouse that eventually became Archie Green's house. Grandma Green just laughed & told me she didn't think I was pregnant. Around Christmas, while decorating at the office of Thunder Bay Mfg., I began to have cramping & spotting, so I went to Dr. Spens to see what was wrong. On his advice, I spent a week doing nothing but lying on the couch with my feet raised by pillows. Again, Grandma was enjoying the "joke". When I went back after that week, he then told me I wasn't & never had been pregnant! I was so embarrassed because I had told everyone. When I asked him why he just shrugged & said I had an "enlarged uterus"! I never went to him again!

I finally convinced Dick that we needed to be on our own & we moved into the little stone house on the mile; between Grandma Green's & Steve Woloszyk. I don't remember how much the rent was, although we had to pay an additional $20 to have an outlet for the electric stove put in. It was only 2-1/2 rooms. The kitchen was at the back with a small pantry. There were no cupboards. We bought an electric stove, a refrigerator, a metal cupboard & a table & chairs. There was a hand pump for water at the sink. It tended to "moan" when it wasn't in use. The "bathroom" was an outhouse about 50 ft. from the back door. Grandma Green gifted me with a porcelain pot with appropriate lid & handle so that I wouldn't need to go outside during the night. The living room was across the front of the house & the "1/2 room" was a long narrow room off the living room, which we utilized as a bedroom – it was just wide enough for a bed to fit tightly, and a rod across the other end made our "closet". We borrowed a daybed from Grandma; put a cover on it & it was our "couch". Various orange crates were utilized as end tables & chairs.

The house was located in an apple orchard & in the fall, apples would fall on the roof, roll off & generally make quite a noise. Janet would stay with us sometimes, but she was afraid of that noise – she never really accepted that it was just apples falling.

I continued to have difficulty with my "periods" & cramping & eventually went to see Dr. Nesbitt who told me the reason for the cramps was my uterus was too small, causing the cramps. He gave me some medication & I got pregnant within a month & never had cramps again. I then went to Dr. O'Donnell, who was an old, partially retired doctor in Alpena & he confirmed that I was really pregnant. He also told me that he wasn't delivering babies any more & suggested I go to Dr. Arscott in Rogers City. I did, and all three of my sons were delivered by him. During the time I was pregnant with Patrick, the draft board contacted Dick & told him his "deferment" was up & he would have to go into the Army. I went to the Board &

told them I was pregnant, due sometime in January of 1955, & asked if he could stay with me until then. They agreed & I promised to let them know as soon as the baby was born. I actually called them from the hospital the day after he was born.

Norvel & Pat had set their wedding day for February 12th & they had a bachelor party on that previous week at our house. I had been to the doctor earlier in the day & he had said I should go in for induced labor since nothing was happening & I was overdue. In order not to pay an extra day's hospital stay, he suggested that I check in after midnight. I had been visiting with some gal pals so I could stay away from the bachelor party; but went home around 11 p.m. & told Dick it was time to go to the hospital. I remember that Edwin Woloszyk was there & he laughed & said I didn't look like I was in labor. Anyway, we left & I checked into the hospital. Dick went back home to finish up the party. There was a snow storm coming & another lady came in early because of it. He came back the next day & stayed with me until the baby was finally born late that afternoon, then went back home to make sure the oil heater was working, and of course went to Norvel & Pat's wedding.

When we came home with the baby I had to learn all sorts of things about taking care of a baby. I had a baby shower in Detroit, given by my old gal pals & a few relatives & had a bottle sterilizer, a couple dozen cloth diapers, a bathinette & a crib. Patrick was born hungry & in the hospital he cried a lot. The nurses put him on his stomach & he would turn his head back & forth until he had rubbed his little nose raw. The comment was made that he looked like a little "pug" when he would move his arms in a boxing manner. He just naturally became Pug & that was his nickname until he started school, when he demanded that nobody call him that anymore.

Dick left for the Army in April of that year, and I was left alone. I knew I couldn't stay in that little stone house & work in Alpena & I had no baby sitter. I remembered my Aunt Lois who never had any kids of her own, but was always taking in other kids. I called & asked if I could come & stay with her & I called Dwight. He came up with a friend & helped me pack up the crib, etc. to move to Dearborn. Norvel & Pat were looking for somewhere to live & moved into the stone house using my "furniture". A year or so later, they moved out & June & Bob Spencer came up with me to clean things out & moved everything into storage in Alpena.

As soon as I moved in with Aunt Lois & Uncle Burl I went back to Kerr Dental Manufacturing to visit & found that my old job was available again. I went right back to work & Aunt Lois & Uncle Burl took care of "Pug" for me. I stayed there while Dick was in the army. When he was in Savannah, Georgia I took some vacation time & went there to visit him before he shipped out to Hawaii where he spent the remainder of his enlistment. It wasn't the hardest life. I had a wonderful baby sitter & a good job that paid well. I received a monthly check from the army & never used the money. I saved it for later & later we surely did need it. I bought a brand new car, a green 1957 Ford.

When Dick was discharged, he immediately wanted to go back to Posen, so I quit my job & we packed up the crib, etc., & went back. We stayed with Grandma & Grandpa Green for a while, but we really needed to get back on our own. We bought a house just off Long Lake. It had a beautiful rock garden separating it from the driveway, which turned out to be full of snakes. One day when I took the garbage out & turned back to the house, I saw a snake crawling out of the rocks in front of me...I got really upset (I am deathly afraid of snakes) & in trying to run across the driveway & up to the house, I fell & skinned my arms, legs, & even my face a little. When Dick came home from work, I was still upset & I was a little hysterical. I told him it was a snake! He thought I had been bitten, but finally we got it straight & decided we had to get rid of the rock garden (& the snakes). He pulled all of the rocks & flowers out – poured kerosene in the holes, & I'm not sure what all, but we did get rid of the snakes.

Another instance there was with Patrick. He was Pug then. He was just a little guy & I would put him in a playpen while I hung clothes out on the line. This day I went with a basket of clothes, glanced in the playpen & there was a very small snake in the playpen with him! I was terrified, but knew I had to do something. I grabbed him out of the pen, took him into the house, got a shovel & ran back – the snake was still there – I killed it with the shovel!

I guess I should explain how Patrick became "Pug". He was hungry when he was born. Just couldn't seem to get enough to eat at the hospital. In the nursery, at that time they always laid the babies on their stomach. He just wouldn't sleep that way, he kept raising his head & moving it back & forth & as a result, he rubbed his little nose raw. To heal it, they gave him something to make him sleep & laid him on his back. His little nose was all raw & as he lay on his back, he moved his arms back & forth in a boxing motion & someone there said he looked like a little Pug (that was a nickname for a prize fighter) & it stuck. When he started school, he asked that no one call him that anymore, & we just got away from it.

While we lived at Long Lake, Pug had a puppy. It was just a skinny little thing – part collie, I think, but he was black & white. He named the dog "98" – I think he picked the name up from a TV commercial at the time for the Oldsmobile 98. Anyway, Larry Filbeck came to visit us. He didn't know where we lived, but remembered that I had bought a new GREEN Ford before I left Dearborn. He went to Posen at the bar & asked about Nancy with a Green Ford, & was told how to find me. He thought the name "98" was really clever for a dog. A few years & 2 kids later, we were visiting in Dearborn – probably at Shelby's, & Larry was there. He picked Karl up, on his knee, & said "Do you-all still have that 98 dog?" Karl looked up at him kind of funny – by that time, we had another dog & he had never known 98. And Karl said "We only have one dog"!

When Aunt Lois died, Grandpa came to the house at Long Lake to tell me. I was very sad & I was lying on the bed crying. Pug (Patrick) came & lay beside me & hugged me & said "That's okay, Mommy, God took Aunt Lois to heaven to take care of Russell". Russell was Norvel & Pat's oldest son who was just 6 months younger than Patrick. He had leukemia & died a few months previously. It seemed that this little boy had things all figured out, & I was surprised that he remembered that Aunt Lois had taken care of him.

Patrick was an inquisitive little guy & always trying to find out what made things work & why, etc. There was one time when he climbed up the TV antenna & got on the roof, but then couldn't get down. I had to get Emmet St. Onge, a neighbor kid to climb up the antenna & get him. Another time, he found a frog & wanted to play with it. I was busy washing clothes at the time & I gave him a small wood plank to put in a washtub filled with water to put the frog on. He had trouble keeping the frog on the plank in the tub; but finally, came to me & said "I fixed it, Momma; now he can't get away". He had found a hammer & nail & had nailed the frog to the plank!

When Grandpa Green was taken to U of M hospital for cancer surgery, I took Grandma down to visit with him. I had to take Patrick with me & when we got to Southfield, I took him to Dad's on Evergreen & asked Jay if she would keep him while we went to Ann Arbor. When I came back by to pick him up, he was very, very unhappy. Jay was obsessed with keeping kids clean & he went outside, as boys will, & got dirty. She stripped his clothes & washed them; in the meantime, putting him in the laundry tub in the Utility Room & scrubbing him down. I think she probably did this more than once while he was there. At any rate, when we got him in the car, he begged, "Please, Momma, don't leave me there anymore – I'm so tired of being clean!"

Another time, when Betty Ann Modrzynski was babysitting & Patrick had started school at Hincks, she called me at work because she had a problem with him. He wouldn't change his underwear to get ready for school. I hadn't told him to do so & I had to tell him on the phone.

Also, at Hincks, when I went to Parent/Teacher day, I was told the teacher had a problem with him because he wouldn't take his cap off for his daily "nap".

After Grandpa died, we decided to sell our house at Long Lake & we bought the farmhouse. Grandma stayed on with us & the kids learned to love her dearly. She would darn their socks when they had holes, & they would thank her, but they wouldn't wear them because of the bumpy feel in their shoes. Even though Grandma was there with them, I always had a baby sitter too. We didn't do a lot of farming, but we did have a few animals, & chickens. Our first chicken when we moved to the farm was a chick Ron Werner had gotten at a gas station at Easter for his kids. He gave it to me to get a livestock start & it grew up to be a rooster & his name was Fletcher. Fletcher was bigger & older than any of the other chickens we had, & he was a pet. He also was mean. Tootsie Misiak would come over with Sandy & Janie & they couldn't get out of the car because Fletcher would jump on the car door handle & peck at the window. He had to be removed & put in the coop while they were visiting. He also attacked the babysitter when she went out to get one of the boys. She actually went to the doctor for treatment where he had torn her forearm with his talons.

There was an incident where the other roosters got together & decided enough was enough. One day they attacked him & the boys found him all beat up & bleeding. They brought him to me crying & asking me to help him. How do you doctor a rooster? Well, I washed him off with alcohol, put a couple of small Band-Aids on the pads of his feet & did the best I could. Then I told them to put him in a separate part of the chicken coop with a couple of hens, until he could heal. He did heal & was meaner than ever. We finally decided we couldn't keep him anymore – he was just too mean! The problem was that after we killed & cleaned him, the kids refused even to try to eat him – He was so tough, I had to boil him all day; but they wouldn't even eat the soup.

There were lots of fun times there on the old farm & I think it was good that the kids had animals. Although sometimes it seemed that instead of farm animals, they were really family pets. Patrick would walk over to Steve & Josie's after school & help Josie with her chores. They raised pigs, in addition to other things & one day he came home & told me that Josie's sow had given birth to piglets & there were too many for the "faucets". He said that Josie had told him that the smallest would die. He asked, "please, Momma" could we take the little ones. We did. Three of them. At that time we had a wood stove in the kitchen & we opened the oven for heat. We put the three tiny little piglets into a large shoebox, with a small doll blanket & set it on the open oven door. They were small enough to hold in one hand & we fed them warm cow's milk with a doll bottle. One of them died the first night, but two lived. They had to be fed frequently – even during the night.

When they outgrew the shoebox, we put them in a box in the shed & started putting Pablum baby food into the milk & finally, oatmeal. They grew fast & soon had to be relegated to the outside buildings. The barnyard was surrounded with an electric fence wire which was about two feet from the ground. The pigs stayed in the barnyard inside the fence so long as we were home. When the kids went off to school & we went to work, they would just walk under the fence & down the road to Steve's, & after school when the kids were home, Steve loaded them on his pickup & brought them home. The kids would play with them in the barnyard & I think they just didn't know they were pigs. Unfortunately, pigs are meant to be food eventually, and that's a fact of life. When it came time for those two pigs to be slaughtered, it was just impossible to think about. We finally found a solution in that we traded those two pigs with Steve for two other ordinary barnyard pigs.

The same sort of thing happened with a calf, the boys had named Goldie. This calf was intended for beef, but by the time it was big enough, they had become attached & we again had to make a trade with Steve. The farm was a source of many fun times. At one time we even had a horse. It was actually Patrick's & he was the only one who rode him. Over the years we had many different dogs, but Pootie & Prince were probably the most memorable. Pootie was a cocker spaniel Josie Woloszyk gave to Patrick & Prince was a German shepherd who was devoted to the boys. Even after the animals were gone, we still enjoyed the property. We accumulated "toys" – a tractor, snowmobiles; (The first was a Skidoo, then a Rupp, & a Skiroule, with an exceptionally wide seat– I was never comfortable riding it.)

To get back to my so-called career choices; I've told you of my first real job at Kerr Manufacturing, but it really wasn't my first. As a teenager, I did some babysitting. At that time we were paid $1.00 until midnight & 25 cents per hour after, so it was a really good job if we got paid $2.00 for a Saturday night. I had one couple who had 2 boys & I sat with them regularly on a weekly basis. That was where I learned to smoke. They were both smokers & would leave butts in the ashtrays. After I got the boys to bed I would light up a butt & smoke it. Eventually, I became a Saturday night smoker. I really didn't buy & smoke my own cigarettes until I was out of school & then I chose Pall Malls.

When I was a junior in high school I answered an ad in the newspaper & got a job that I thought was taking care of a couple of boys when they came home from school until their parents came from work. They were Jewish & I earned $10 a week by going after school (around noon) to their house, by bus & working until 5 p.m. It totaled about 4 hours a day for 5 days a week & until the boys came from school, my duties included vacuuming, dusting, mopping, washing clothes & even cleaning a fireplace in the living room. I still considered myself a babysitter until one day one of the boys was on a "field" trip with his class & brought them, with their teacher to his home to meet his "Maid"! Then, I quit.

In my senior year, I needed money for graduation stuff – dress, shoes, etc., & all the things that go with it. I know my dad would have given me money if I had asked, but I never wanted to ask for anything. There was a neighbor who had a dry-cleaning business & he specialized in repairing oriental rugs. I worked for him (at home) removing the fringe of worn oriental rugs, so that he could repair & re-fringe them. I earned 35 cents per yard – about $1.40 for one side of a 12 ft. rug. My fingers would be very raw after working, but I managed to pay for my graduation stuff.

After graduation, as I said, I went to work as Secretary to the Sales Manager, Harry Lange, at Kerr Manufacturing Company in Detroit. It was very interesting work, & I was pretty good at my job. They came out with a robo-type machine at that time. It was an electric typewriter that you could type a letter on, putting in stops for the name & address, as well as possible personal inserts in the body of the letter. Our typewriters at that time were all manual except for this one. This was quite the invention. After I moved to Posen, my first instinct was to try to get a job with a dentist since I knew all about dental supplies, etc.; however, I went to work at Montgomery Ward instead. Then, as I said, I went on to work for the foundry in Alpena until Patrick was born.

When I went back to Detroit to get a job, I was fortunate enough to go back to work at the same job as Secretary to Harry Lange at Kerr. When Dick came home from the army, we came back up north. Reuben Bruning decided to open an electric supply store in Rogers City & I went to work for him. I set up his books & worked in the store with one of the Karstens until Scott was born. Dick later began working for Reuben & eventually went to classes to obtain his electrician's license so he could work at Stoneport. But, again, I digress.

Jerry Bruning came up & took over the bookkeeping at the store (Northern Electric) & I began looking for work in Alpena. I answered an ad in the paper & after interviews with Chub White & Ron Werner, went to work for Fletcher Paper Company in 1960. The original job was to be working with orders as they intended to transfer the Chicago office to Alpena, but it fell through at the time, so I was called in to fill in for vacations that summer. I worked two weeks in July filling in for the girl who typed orders, and then while waiting for someone else to go on vacation, I worked for Chub White. He had just started working the year before & didn't have a secretary or anyone to take care of his correspondence, etc. I spent that summer cleaning up the past year's work & setting up his files. A new automated system had been ordered & was due to be installed in the fall. In October, Ann whom I had replaced in July, had a stroke & never returned to work. Therefore, I ended up working on the installation of the new Friden, Punch-Tape Automatic Order/Acknowledgement system.

It was a "touchy" thing & needed more than one person to learn the operation, so after some interviews, Donnaleen Burke was hired (again part-time) to learn & help me out. It became a 30-yr working friendship. Donna's husband was also named Dick & we had fun referring to her Dick & my Dick. She had a son, Michael, who was just a yr or two older than Patrick & we all became friends. As I mentioned, I was a smoker at the time, & it was kind of "cool" to be a smoker. Donna never smoked at work, but at noon I would sometimes go home with her for lunch & it was quite the trip! As she walked in the kitchen door, she would kick off her shoes, & by the time she got to the living room, her dress was dropped & she was in her slip. Then she would light a cigarette, hold it gingerly, puff & blow smoke out; all very quickly like her life depended on it. It was really a funny site. Then after a quick sandwich or cup of soup for lunch, it went in reverse, & she was back fully dressed, shoes & all & in the car going back to work!

There were many good times at Fletcher's; eventually, I became Manager of Administration & Donna worked up to Office Manager. That was the time when everything in Alpena shut down on Wednesday afternoons for golf for the guys! I had never golfed, but Donna did & she kept after me to give it a try, until finally I gave in & it's been a part of my life ever since.

Fletcher leased a plane from Welch Aviation for business trips, etc. & at the end of the year, there generally was flying time left on the lease. We girls in the office were given the opportunity to take the plane & go wherever we decided we wanted to go – it was usually in December. One was a memorable trip to Chicago where we went to meet all the crew there & to bring Anita Soik back home for Christmas. In Chicago we did some very interesting & amusing site-seeing. Marge & Kay had never seen an Escalator before & needless to say, Neeman-Marcus had never experienced the Fletcher Gals before either!

The thirty years at Fletcher were very gratifying. I had a good job with a lot of responsibility & I worked for a man, Chub White, whom I admired greatly. After Chub's retirement, it was never the same, & I made the decision to also retire early, along with Donnaleen, Ron Werner, & Herb Markham. After we left, things really changed, & the company went bankrupt, leaving a bad taste for everyone. I will always be grateful to the Fletcher family for my experiences & my retirement.

I always thought when I retired I would have nothing to do, & I had helped Teri Romel get a business started in Alpena, whereby, vacations & time off could be replaced with temporary employees trained & ready to go to work. It was my intention to work for "The Secretarial Pool" when I retired; but somehow I never found the time. I was introduced to the AARP Tax Aide Program by Dennis Artley in 1989 & have been working with the group ever since. We help older citizens & low income people file taxes. This year (2010) I am responsible for 9 sites, from Oscoda & Tawas to Presque Isle & across to Hale & Rose City. We e-file, utilizing 4 desktop computers, and 15 laptops, as well as a number of printers, for which I am held responsible.

In addition, I have volunteered at the Elks Lodge in Alpena as Secretary & Treasurer for a number of years. I have also been at various times, President of the golf league at both the Alpena Golf Club as well as the former Alpena Country Club. I am still doing the job of Tournament Chairperson at the Golf Club. I served on the Board at the Country Club for a couple of years, & have been (still am) Secretary on the Alpena Golf Club Board. I've also at various times served on the board of the Bowling Leagues. While working I was on the United Way Board, as well as the Alpena Chamber of Commerce; and also a member of Zonta.

When I originally came to Posen, the Posen Potato Festival was born (1952). During those early years, I enjoyed it along with everyone else. As time went on, I became involved in the initiation of the Posen Queen's Pageant. Prior to that time, the queen was selected by selling lottery tickets. I mentioned at a pre-festival meeting that I didn't think that was right; & was then given the job of doing it differently. I headed up the pageant & worked with the queens from 1968 until 1982 when I moved to Alpena. In addition to the Pageant, I also served on the Chamber of Commerce in Posen as Secretary & as its first woman president. I was asked to head up the queen's pageant in Onaway & got it off to a successful start. Around that same time, I also helped to get the Rogers City Queen's Pageant going. I was asked to judge at many other pageants around the area – Mackinac City – Alpena's Jr. Miss – as well as the Miss Alpena Pageant. It was a fun time.

At the time I started the Pageant, there was a "crackdown" in Michigan on unlicensed lotteries. Each year the C of C would purchase some large item (car, guns, etc.) & sell tickets for a chance to win it. The tickets were mostly sold by the 16 & 17-yr old girls who were vying for queen. Although the C of C accepted my idea of a pageant, the girls were still selling tickets. Originally, five girls were voted on from the senior class at the high school to participate in the pageant. One of them had relatives living in Gaylord & approached a neighbor there to purchase a ticket. It just happened that he was an off-duty State Policeman, and he made a report of the "illegal lottery". Nothing was done that year to stop the pageant, or the festival. After a successful pageant & festival, I was then elected President of the C of C.

The following year, I was in the Post Office, placing pictures of the queen candidates, etc in the window when I was approached by a Rogers City Police Officer (Walter Kelly, I think) & he gave me a summons for a court appearance that week. Yes, we were taken to court on a charge of running an illegal lottery. As the current President, I was the main defendant, but the new Secretary, Elmer Kamyszek, was also called. He had been given a briefcase by the former Secretary, Bole Centala, but had no idea of what was in it. It was almost comical as he sat in the witness chair with the briefcase at his feet & when asked questions, answered by pointing to the case & stating "it's all in there". Harlan Addison had consulted an Alpena attorney & maintained that since no one knew where the drawing was held, there was no lottery. I think the trial went on for at least 2 or 3 days & there wasn't a doubt in anyone's mind that we had run a lottery without a license. We were, of course, found guilty by then Judge Glennie; but there were no consequences since we were no longer doing the lottery, & we were set free to get back to the business of running the festival.

When we returned to Posen, we were told that a state inspector had been at the hall & had banned the use of all of the pots & pans used for the potato pancake dinner. I was introduced to him & he told me he was a Baptist minister & an inspector in his spare time. He explained that the enamel cookware was no longer allowed & that we needed stainless steel cookware. He wished us good luck & said he would be back on Sunday to enjoy the pancakes. Ha! Now we really had a problem – we couldn't just go ahead with what we had because he might really come back. We considered borrowing from the Church or the school but they were also using enamel at that time. Then someone said "Where do we get enough pots & pans to feed an army?" Then I knew what to do. I had a friend who was an army recruiter & had access to the armory in Alpena. I called him, made arrangements to borrow stainless steel pots & pans from the army – One of Styma's potato trucks was sent to Alpena, and we were back in business! I don't know if the inspector showed up on Sunday or not – I was too busy elsewhere.

There were many other interesting happenings during my tenure with the Chamber of Commerce. For the Centennial, I was one of a 3-person group (Barb Ennest & Ruby Klimaszewski) who put together the Centennial Book. We went all over the county interviewing people of interest & gathering old pictures. I still have a copy, and I'm proud to say, I think it makes very interesting reading. The Posen Cookbook was also one of my ventures. A group of us gathered together & obtained recipes from local Polish & German cooks. I enlisted the help of Roger Dahl at Fletcher to draw a picture for the front cover, & I typed all the recipes, adding little drawings for the divisions & the Fletcher Printers printed the recipes on the then new colored paper. I borrowed a machine for the binding from Young & Nethercutt & gathered a group of high school kids at the gym & we collated the books & they went on sale. They were so successful that the following year, we were able to have them re-printed professionally.

Also, for the centennial I obtained a pattern for an old fashioned bathing suit & cap, as well as a man's vest, and I sewed the bathing suits for all of the girls in the pageant to wear in their fitness number on stage. It was a fun time, with all the local guys growing beards & the women making & wearing old-fashioned dresses. I had an idea & talked to several of the ladies about it & we put on a fashion show featuring fashions of 100 years. As entertainment I also wrote a little skit based on the dying swan, but used local guys dressed in tights & tutus. It was a hilarious success!

I just remembered my very first vacation after beginning work at Kerr & I'll tell you about it. I was 19 yrs old & felt like I knew everything! I made plans to travel to Kentucky & visit family. I lived with Dwight & Janie at that time on Acacia in Detroit. I bought a ticket for a bus to Mayfield Kentucky. I was to board the bus at the corner of Grand River & Schoolcraft. I bought a small suitcase & a matching carry-on. A few days before I was scheduled to leave, I received a phone call from the bus company. They told me there was a little girl (10 yrs. Old) who was going to the same destination in KY & her parents asked if I could "escort" her. Of course! I was an adult & I knew what I was doing. They brought her to the bus stop just a little before we were scheduled to leave & I assured them that everything would be okay. Oh, how very adult & smart I felt!

We sat together on the bus & when we stopped to eat or for breaks, etc. on the way down, I kept a close eye on her & we did just fine. It was a very long trip – I don't remember how many hours, but it took all day before we got into Paducah where we had to change buses. As we left the bus, I watched carefully to see where our suitcases went – that's how you know where to go, right? Well, our suitcases were put on a bus which had a sign reading "Fulton"; but that's okay, I'm with the suitcases! Before we left, the bus driver took a head count & confirming that he had the right amount of passengers, we took off. We sat immediately behind the driver, & I carried on a conversation with him, learning about the cities we were traveling through. We made several stops, & as fewer & fewer people were left; he asked me about our destination. I told him we were going to Mayfield & he became very excited. The bus emptied out at Fulton & that was the end of the line! It seems there were two small Negro children asleep on a seat in the back of the bus, & the driver missed them when he counted heads in Paducah! This bus didn't even go to Mayfield!

He took us inside the bus station & treated us to supper at the restaurant while he called his superiors to see what to do. When he called, he found that my grandfather, as well as the little girl's grandparents were frantically searching for us at the bus station in Mayfield. We got back on the bus & he drove us to the station in Mayfield where we met our anxious grandparents. I was just a little embarrassed when the little girl told her grandparents she was so glad I was with her, because without me she wouldn't have known what to do. I thought to myself that without me she would have been on the right bus – but of course, I just graciously accepted her thanks!

Aside from the trip down, my visit was very enjoyable. One thing that stands out was when I visited with Aunt Nellie. My cousin, Larry couldn't have been more than 14 or 15 at the time, & he & a friend (Trellis Gore) took me out on the town. The entire county was dry, but we drove across the Tennessee border & went to a town I remember as DumBarque where we found a bar with music & dancing. I learned all the words to "Down Yonder" & learned to dance a Kentucky Jig. Trellis could really move his feet. I found out later, he wasn't interested in me, but was trying to impress Larry because he was interested in Aunt Nellie!

I think I may have been practicing for my later trip to KY when I drove down in my little blue caddy that I mentioned earlier; because there was another time I went astray on a KY trip. Earl Koss was in the Army & stationed at Fort Knox. He came home for Christmas with the family, but didn't make round-trip reservations for some reason. Grandpa Koss (Stanley) had a new Dodge at time (it had a pushbutton starter & door lock) & he offered to let me drive it to take Earl back. I took time off work & Pat Koss & Edna joined me on the trip. It proved to be a great adventure! I was driving with Earl in the front & the 2 girls in the back. The trip was uneventful until we reached the bridge over Kentucky Lake at Paducah! I was following a map & had no idea until I rounded a curve & there it was! It seemed like the biggest & scariest suspension bridge I had ever seen & everyone was asleep! I yelled out for them to wake up, but even awake, there was no help! I was already on the bridge – I told them to talk to me – not about the bridge – anything else…finally, when I got across, I had nail marks in both hands from holding so tightly to the steering wheel & I was shaking, but I made it!

The rest of the trip down was just an ordinary drive. We arrived at my Uncle Joe's & my cousin, Joe Neal took Earl out for the evening & we dropped him off at Fort Knox the next day. We made a big deal of saying goodbye to him in front of his fellow soldiers, pretending that we were all girlfriends. Then came the trip back. We drove all day & somewhere we got lost. It became dark & we could see the lights indicating an expressway, but we kept driving in circles & just couldn't get there. All the time, it seems the radio just kept playing "Downtown" – where we really wanted to go! Finally, we pulled over & stopped a semi & asked the driver to help us. He told us to follow him & we did – to a motel, where he told us we should get a room for the night so we could start fresh the next day. We did & the next day we found that we were within blocks of the right route – just couldn't see it.

Many times I have pondered about how I ended up here in Northern Michigan. With most of my family in Kentucky, some moving to Dearborn & some moving back to Kentucky, how did I manage to find this place where I plan to live out the rest of my life? I think I mentioned earlier how I met Dick Green. He apparently moved to Southfield to live with his Aunt Doris & Reuben Bruning while attending high school at Highland Park. He didn't finish school, but went to work at Fabristeel, a small machine shop on Eight Mile Rd. He worked with Dolores Wilkinson, who was a sister to my best friend, June. The Wilkinsons lived on a farm on Evergreen, across the road from my Dad's. It wasn't a large farm, but it was a farm & they had rabbits, chickens & various other animals. It's kind of hard to imagine that now, but at the time, Southfield was country.

I had moved out of Dad's & was living with Dwight & Jane, but always went back to Southfield & Wilkinsons on the weekends. I believe I related the story earlier about passing out dates one afternoon at the farm; and that Dick actually showed up. We didn't live on Acacia very long & our next move was to the old neighborhood in Southfield. The house was on the street right behind Bruning's building. The day we moved in, we were all busy putting things away & Jane was working in the living room when she heard something & saw Dick looking in the window! She was surprised & let out a screech! He came in, helped us move things around & then came back almost on a daily basis. In fact, when I got off the bus at Southfield & Eight Mile, he would be there to pick me up after work. We never went anywhere except to the Wilkinson farm, or just stayed home & played checkers. We did go to the movies once. He came over & told me Bob Westermeier wanted to go to the show & he asked me to go too. I may even have paid my own way – I don't remember.

He told me about his family & his previous engagement & we became very close. He got his draft notice the same day we decided to get married. I've told you of our trip to Kentucky with Dwight when my grandmother Patton was sick. After we came back, we started to make plans for our wedding, to be held in Posen. We drove up to Posen so that I could meet his family & I've already told you of those experiences. We were very much in love & although there were some rough times, we had some very good times too. Our life in the little stone house before he went to the army was all about fun! We had a black & white collie dog named Daffy, but I don't remember what happened to him. Dick left for the Army a couple of months after Patrick was born & I don't think he ever thought about being a father.

During the time he was in the Army, while I was living with Aunt Lois, I made it a priority to tell Pug all about his dad. I had a picture of him in uniform & I let Pug carry it around in his walker & he kept it with him all the time – this was his "daddy". One day we were going to the corner drugstore & as I drove up & parked. I went around the side to take him out of the car, set him down on the sidewalk & turned to shut the car door. He took off running after a young man in uniform, grabbed him around the leg & cried, "Daddy, Daddy, Daddy". I was so embarrassed & apologized to the young soldier, explaining to him that his dad was in the army. The young man was very kind, but it was difficult explaining to Pug that not everyone in uniform was "daddy".

When Dick was discharged, I don't think it took more than a day for him to make sure we were all packed up & ready to leave for Posen – He wanted to get "home". His relationship with Patrick just wasn't what it should have been. He seemed to think that this little boy should be all grown up. He never picked him up & never hugged him. He just thought he was a helper, to run errands, etc. He missed out on all of the baby stuff. When Scott was born, it was like that was his first-born. He always seemed to prefer Scott – even after Karl came along. When we were living at the farm in Posen, Dick would often go out drinking after work. Generally, I would put his supper in the oven & leave it on warm, so he had something to eat when he came home. When he did come home, he would take his supper out of the oven, & call for Scott to come sit with him while he ate. Scott would wake up & come out & sit with him & listen to him until he finally would go to bed. When something needed to be done around the farm, Dick would tell Scott about it & usually after school, Patrick or Karl would see that the chore was done & when Dick came home, he never acknowledged them. It has always been amazing to me that both Patrick & Karl seemed to understand that & haven't held it against Scott.

While living at Long Lake we met different friends, but still had the old friends from Posen. We went out on Saturday nights as a rule. The Deer Hunt Inn, Melody Inn (Red Top) - Now Kelly's Venture Inn, & occasionally Three Pines Tavern, Hideaway Inn, or the Posen Pub. Sometimes we would even go as far as Gaylord for a Saturday night. I loved to dance & at that time Dick drank only beer & he could drink all evening without getting obnoxious. It wasn't until he started drinking R & R that he began to be hard to live with. It wasn't unusual to have a large group of friends over for dinner & finish up with an evening of playing cards. We spent many of our evenings playing cards, either with friends or just the two of us. We enjoyed each other's company & had much to talk about.

Our 25th Wedding Anniversary was a cause for celebration. I had always thought we might go to Hawaii where Dick had spent his service time; but he wanted to have a big celebration with all of his friends. It turned out quite nice. Friends & relatives from Southfield came up & we all had a great time.

When Scott & Karl decided to get married, it turned into one of the biggest weddings Posen had ever seen. It was almost like 2 separate weddings, rolled into one day. The girls had different friends & different tastes. Each chose different colors & each had their own attendants. It was quite a day. With all the visiting relatives, both the farmhouse & the trailer at the lake were filled with visitors & Dick & I ended up sleeping in the camper in the driveway at the farm. After we were settled in, I began to feel the loss – no more kids at home! I began to cry & Dick asked me what was wrong – I said "They're all gone!" & couldn't hold back the tears – I suddenly felt so lonesome. He just looked at me, laughed & said, "They'll be back". He never understood. Karl & Cheri were living in Detroit & Scott moved down to Texas; Patrick & Paulette were living at Grand Lake; & we were suddenly left with no one at home. I think that may have been when I really became aware of how much he was drinking & how it was affecting us. It seemed that anytime we went anywhere he ended up drunk. It just wasn't fun anymore.

We still had parties & we still had friends over on weekends, but it wasn't the same. Maybe he needed having the kids around to complain to & about – I really don't know, but it became really hard to come home from work & be in the house with just the two of us. It all came to a head in July of 1982. We went to a July 4th celebration at the Presque Isle Lighthouse & park. There was a picnic & a band for dancing, etc. A good time was had by all, but eventually, it became time to go home. The Reisner's were there & invited us to their cottage across the lake to play cards. Dick was already drunk & wanted to go, but I said no & drove us home. At that time, I had a problem with my car & was driving a loaner from McCoys & needed gas to get to town. When we got home I left to get gas & then drove down to the opening & just parked for a while to give him time to get to sleep as I didn't want to argue. When I got home he was asleep & I went to bed without incident. In the morning I got up, made breakfast & his lunch & sent him off to work. Then went back to bed before having to get up & go to work myself. The phone woke me up. It was Patrick & he asked what had gone on that night. Apparently, while I was gone, Dick had called Scott in Texas & told him I had left him & he had his pistol & was going to shoot me & himself. Scott then called Patrick. That was when I decided I had to leave.

I went to work with no intention of going home. Strangely enough, my job was taking care of personnel problems & that very day one of the employees called & asked to talk to me. He wanted to know what to do, as his wife had just left him. Talk about Karma! I advised him to talk to her & find out what the problem was & try to get into counseling. Previously, I had asked Dick to go to counseling & he refused. At any rate, now I had my own problems to deal with. I don't remember if I called him or he called me at work, but I did tell him I was coming to get some clothes, but was not coming home. I called Pat & asked him to go with me. I thought it might avoid an out & out fight.

We sat at the table & I told him that he absolutely could not call the boys with our problems & make such threats about killing. He said he was only fooling around & didn't mean it. I took a few of my clothes & left, telling him I would talk to him later about what we would do. I went to the Fletcher Motel & stayed the night. The next day I picked up my own car & began to try to figure out what I could do. I called Dan White, Chub

White's son, who was an attorney & asked about filing for divorce. He told me I would have to establish at least a 2 wk residency in Alpena County, or else file in Rogers City. I found out that Jean Guy (who had previously divorced Allan) was living with someone & her daughter was in her house. I called & asked if I could move in for a couple of weeks & she agreed. I stayed there for a couple of weeks & during that time began searching for a place to really live. I looked at apartments in Alpena, most generally old homes which had been converted. One, in particular, was really dreary – the laundry was in a dark basement & I mostly found nothing until I found an ad for a furnished apartment in Ossineke.

I moved into that upstairs furnished apartment & went back to the lake & took a few dishes & pans & towels. I asked for my chair & the bedroom TV but didn't take them at the time. The Farleys came to visit me with Dick & brought the TV. Although it was a nice apartment, it was strange using someone else's furniture. I met several times with Dan White & he made all the arrangements for the divorce. Dick refused to get his own lawyer & met with me & Dan personally. The distribution of assets wasn't too difficult, since I was taking nothing but my car & clothes. The difficult part was the properties. The farm had already been sold & the house & property in Texas had been paid for with the proceeds. A lot had been separated for Karl & he had a trailer on it. We managed to get the house separated from the land & put the house in Scott's name, with the land going to Karl. The house at the lake was put in a joint tenancy between Pat & Dick with full rights to the survivor. There was just around $2600 left on the mortgage at that time. I paid up all the insurances to date – my car, Dick's car (remember the red Pontiac), his pickup, etc. The Pontiac was also paid up, as well as the pontoon, the tractor, the dump truck & the van. He was left with literally everything paid up to the next month's utilities & the balance on the house.

I was left with my paycheck & an empty checkbook; but I knew I could make it. I was hoping he would be okay too – If he could just keep his job. The divorce was final on October 2, 1982 & took only about 10 minutes in the courthouse. I left the courthouse, drove over to the fairgrounds, parked & cried. But life goes on & it did.

That was my last year working on the Posen pageant & festival. I turned the pageant reigns over to the former pageant queens & apparently they have done just fine. I haven't been to a Potato Festival since then, but it goes on successfully each year without me. Someone once told me if you begin to feel that you are indispensible, just put your fist in a bucket of water, imagine it's you in the world – take it out & see how much you are missed!

I was learning to be independent. I had been having some problems with my Pontiac & decided to look at another car. I went to Anscheutz & saw a white Z-28 Camaro in the showroom. It had a removable roof & seemed to be just the kind of thing I needed. I bought a couple of ABBA tapes, put them in on high & drove around with my neck scarf flying in the wind. I was 50, single & wild!

I became friends with the couple next door, Sam & Peggy. She was his second wife & she was not well. His kids didn't like her & never came to visit. I liked them both, & sometimes would make enough dinner to take it to them. One Thanksgiving, I slipped on the step in front of their door & spilled cornbread dressing all over – managed to save enough for dinner, though. When she died, he asked me to find someone to buy her engagement ring because he didn't want his daughter to have it. I bought her ring & his too & ended up with some other things when his daughter had a yard sale. The black marble-topped table came from them, a brass lamp (now in the basement), as well as a few pictures that I thought were nice.

As I accumulated enough money to buy some furniture, I moved from the upstairs apartment to a two-bedroom up & down. It was really nice to be able to have my own things again, and as time went on I was able to move out of the apartment into my own Condo at Village Green. It was almost identical to the apartment, except that I owned it rather than paying rent. Of course, I didn't really own it – I borrowed the down payment from my 401K & financed the rest at the bank, but it was mine. When I retired in 1989-90 I had to pay the interest on the 401K loan & Fletcher kept me on as a consultant until I was 59-1/2 so that I didn't have to pay the penalty. I will always be grateful to Fletcher for my retirement. I wasn't old enough to draw Social Security, so I used money from my 401K to supplement my pension & pay for my travelling life-style. And, travel, I did.

I went on several bus trips with Jeff Welch & Rainbow Tours – The Grand Ole Opry – Atlantic City – Washington, DC – Toronto – The Grand Canyon & Mt. Rushmore. I went to Golf school in Indiana. I went to St. Kitts in November on a golfing holiday (annually, for a number of years). I flew to Vegas almost every year until the casinos became the big thing in Michigan. There were bowling trips to Reno & California, Wisconsin, Florida & other places I've forgotten. I went to Texas to visit Scott & Karl & their families. I drove down to Kentucky, Texas & Florida. I went to Florida for a couple of weeks in the winter – I went to Hawaii. I even had one very memorable trip to Germany with my now deceased buddy, Maria. I will always remember that trip & what I learned. I'm settled down now, and not in any hurry to travel anywhere – I'm enjoying my life here in Alpena too much. Oh, I'll probably take a trip or two to Texas before I give up entirely & I may even go to the

East Coast some time, but right now I'm perfectly happy right here.

Lately, I've been in touch with some long-lost relatives in Kentucky (by way of the computer) & I may make another trip there someday. I hope my sons will stay in touch with some of the Pattons, the Filbecks & the Barkers – and let the legend live on.

The Barkers – Now, I feel I have to explain. Kelly Barker was my mother's second husband & my stepfather. I've told you he had 2 other children when they married & how Norman & Shelby were born. Well, after Mom died & we moved out, Kelly married Edith (the baby sitter). They had three other children, Judy, Bobbi, & Richard; who were half-brothers & sister to Norman & Shelby, although no relation to me & Dwight. However, as I said, Dwight & I stayed in touch with Norman & Shelby & after Kelly died, & the kids all got older, it seemed that our families kind of melded together. Judy & her husband came with Shelby to visit us at the lake, & as a result their kids became friends with our boys. So – there is the other extended family!

I'm including some ancestry information on my family which I've accumulated on the computer. Julian (Bongo) Hoppe is working on the Koss's, the Greens, the Sommerfields & the Neumanns. When it's finished, I will get copies for you.

Ancestors of Nancy J Patton Green
b. April 9, 1932 in Detroit, MI

Parents

1. Orvice Monroe Patton, b 28 May 1907 Calloway County KY d. Jan 1980 Oakland County MI. He married (1) Trema Lillian Filbeck 27 Feb 1926 Marshall County KY b. May 13, 1909 Marshall County KY d 13 Dec 1943 Wayne County MI. He married (2) Julia Ann Zimmerman Barbowski 1937 b. 12 Mar 1907 Pennsylvania, d 16 Dec 1999 Oakland County, MI

   Children by Trema Lillian Filbeck:
   a. Nancy Jane Patton, b Apr 9 1932 Detroit, MI. Married Richard James Green, 2/23/52
   b. Dwight Leroy Patton, b Jan 2, 1927 Marshall County KY. Married (1) Jane Serra 1951, b 1929 d 1968. Married (2) Gloria 1978 b 1926

2. Trema Lillian Filbeck, b May 13, 1909 Marshall County, KY d 13 d 1943 Wayne County MI She married (2) Kelly Barker, 1937 by 12 Aug 1902 d 22 Nov 1957

   Children by Kelly Barker:
   a. Norman Roger Barker, b 1 Feb 1939 Wayne County. Married Marian ??
   b. Shelby Joan Barker, b 10 Jan 1940 Married (1) Doran Manus 1957 b 1936 d. 1990. Married (2) Al Fernandez 2001 Dearborn, MI
   c. Baby Barker, Stillborn Oct 1943 Wayne Co. MI

Grand Parents

3. <u>Willard Oetis Patton,</u> b 9 Jul 1885 Calloway Co. KY d 22 Aug 1965. Married <u>Hattie Elizabeth Turnbow</u> 1905
4. <u>Lonnie Filbeck,</u> b 2 Aug 1883, d 4 Nov 1961. Married <u>Nancy Lee Magness</u> 17 Jul 1904

Great Grand Parents

5. <u>James Monroe Patton,</u> b 24 Apr 1854 Calloway Co., KY d 12 May 1928. Married <u>Matilda Frances Langston.</u>
6. <u>Amos Jefferson Turnbow,</u> b 2 Jun 1861 KY d 1931. Married <u>Sophronia Jane Harris.</u>
7. <u>James Levi Filbeck,</u> b 16 Jun 1859 Marshall Co. KY. Married <u>Violia I. Barnett</u> 13 Jan 1880.
8. <u>Josiah James (Joe) Magness,</u> b 7 Aug 1837, d 12 Dec 1912. Married (1) <u>Barbara Elizabeth Baker</u> Married <u>(2) Nancy L. Wrather,</u> d 10 Dec 1876. Married <u>(3) S. F. Jones</u> 2 Mar 1908

Great Great Grand Parents

9. <u>Thomas Patton,</u> b 1832 North Carolina, d 1932 Calloway Co. KY. Married <u>Marjorie J. McCallom</u> 1852
10. <u>William B. Langston,</u> b 19 Jun 1827 Calloway Co. KY, d 11 Sep 1905. Married <u>Dulaney Lynch</u> 19 Nov 1852
11. <u>Lewis Presley Turnbow,</u> b 1836 KY, d 1864. Married Pauline Tiny Armstrong.
12. <u>James A. Filbeck,</u> b 1823 Shelby NC. Married <u>Malinda Jane Goheen,</u> 8 Apr 1852 Marshall Co. KY
13. <u>Zachariah Magness.</u> Married <u>Mary Frances Ragsdale</u> 18 Dec 1828 Williamson Co. Tenn.

14. <u>Peter B. Baker</u> d 6 Nov 1887. Married <u>???</u> Alcock, 26 Feb 1879.

3rd Great Grand Parents

15. <u>??? Patton</u>. Married <u>Elizabeth Wilson</u>. Only son Thomas Patton
15. <u>Luke Langston, b 20 Apr 1794 NC d 26 Dec 1873 Calloway Co</u>. KY. Married Jerusha Knight.
16. <u>Thomas Jefferson Turnbow</u>. B 26 May 1814 Alabama, d 11 Aug 1891 Graves KY. Married (1) <u>Rachel Shultz</u>, b 9 Aug 1812 Indiana. Married (2) <u>Betsey Whitt Ward</u>.
17. <u>John Philbeck</u> –
18. <u>James E. Goheen, 3rd</u>. b. 21 Feb 1808 Sumner Co. TN, d 10 July 1870 Marshall Co. KY. Married <u>Elizabeth Utley</u> 4 Feb 1830 Logan KY.

4th Great Grand Parents

19. <u>Stephen Turnbow</u>, b 7 Jun 1792 in KY d. 21 Jul 1860. Married <u>Mary Clapp</u> 11 Aug 1813 Madison, Alabama
20. <u>William Felbach</u>. B 16 Mar 1772
21. <u>James Goheen Jr.</u> b abt 1768. Married <u>Mary Pinkston</u> Rowan Co. NC
22. <u>Merrill Utley</u>, b 5 Aug 1777. Married <u>Winifred Jones</u> 8 Dec 1800 Wake Co. NC

5th Great Grand Parents

23. <u>Isaac Turnbow</u>, b about 1762 Perry Co. Al., d 11 Jun 1829. Married <u>Margaret Tallkitten</u>.
24. Luddwick Lewis Clapp. Married <u>Margaret Ann Loye</u>.

25. <u>Wilhelm Ernest Felbach</u> b 1728 Wiesbaden, Germany d 1801 Union County, SC – Marrried ??
26. <u>James Goheen, Sr.</u> b Abt 1740, d 26 Apr 1796. Married <u>Elizabeth ??</u> Rowan NC
27. <u>Jacob Utley</u>, b about 1752. Married <u>Phoebe sanders</u>.

6th Great Grand Parents

28. <u>John Andrew Turnbow</u>, b about 1737 or 1740. Married <u>Marget ??</u>
29. <u>Isaac Tallkitten</u> – married ???